Authored By: Ayna Miah

TABLE OF CONTENTS

FOREWORD

What is a stockbroker? There are many answers to that question. First, a stockbroker buys and sells stocks on behalf of their clients or their firm. A stockbroker is also an advisor, a researcher, a compiler of investment information, and a sales person. A stockbroker can also be a support mechanism to a new public company or an old Fortune 100 company.

A stockbroker works under the regulation of the Security and Exchange Commission (SEC) of the United States, if they are in the United States. They are regulated on how they can offer stock, how they must treat their client's transactions, and only by passing the tests of the SEC can they do business.

To the client a stockbroker can be a "financial friend", or a client's worst enemy. It all depends on the nature of the stockbroker, their honesty, and adherence to the regulations that they must follow.

Almost everyone knows something about the stock market. Some know from activities that reach the major news outlets regarding violations of rules or tenets of the marketplace. Occasionally a stockbroker is disciplined by the SEC, or charged by a court of competent jurisdiction for legal wrongdoing. Some know from major events in the stock market, i.e. the crash of '29, the dot com bubble, and other events.

What can becoming a stockbroker do for you? You can serve your fellow man. You can learn a living. You can become very wealthy. You can grow and go on to become the principle in your own stock brokerage company.

A career as a stockbroker must start with proper licensing. To become licensed you must pass at least two tests a Series 6, and a Series 7. If you work for a firm and advance you career up the ladder there are other tests that must be passed, i.e. Broker Principle, before you can do that job.

Being a stockbroker offers all the challenges of an important sales position. You must be a specialist before you can begin to do the work that produces your income and provide the vital services your clients expect. Once prepared you job is to provide your clients access to a wide variety of markets such as the New York Stock Exchange, the American Stock Exchange, NASDAQ, several commodity exchanges such as the Chicago Exchange, and specialized insurance and banking products as well.

If one thing can be said about becoming a stockbroker it is that it is not easy. The job changes with the whims and wills of the regulators, volatile conditions in the economy and marketplace, and the idiosyncrasies of individual human beings. Becoming a stockbroker requires dedication and the ability to learn and evolve with the times and the financial environment.

INTRODUCTION

This book will attempt to provide you with a comprehensive overview of the stockbroker. It cannot be the definitive work on the subject, as that would take much more space and memory than anyone would desire.

We will discuss the required licensing, the appropriate laws that you need to know in your investigation of the career, what types of stocks, bonds, funds, and other financial instruments that are pertinent, and what your potential clients will likely expect from you.

We invite you to enjoy this book with the understanding that it can only be a starting point on your journey to becoming a licensed and official stockbroker. We invite you to research on your own from what you learn here to gain a better and full understanding of what is involved in person a stockbroker.

WHAT IS THE STOCK MARKET

When you hear the term "stock market," you might think of big business, big bucks, and wheeler-dealers making big deals. All that may seem far removed from your daily life.

The purpose of a stock exchange is to facilitate the exchange of securities between buyers and sellers, thus providing a marketplace (virtual or real). Just imagine how difficult it would be to sell shares (and what a disadvantage you would be at with respect to the buyer) if you had to call around trying to locate a buyer.

In reality the stock market affects you in ways you may never notice. Say, for example, that Uncle Fred's restaurant chain wants to build more restaurants or add an oyster bar to its restaurants. It takes money to buy land, build restaurants, and develop and advertise new menu items.

If Uncle Fred's doesn't have all the money it needs in its own pockets, it sells shares to investors through a stock market. By buying a share, each investor owns a piece of Uncle Fred's. As owners, stockholders receive company information and can attend the annual meeting, where they vote on company issues. The number of shares of stock a person owns is the number of votes he or she may cast.

Thousands of companies do the same thing to raise the money they need to do whatever they do and make whatever they make. If the stock market were to shut down completely tomorrow, those companies wouldn't be able to sell shares. And then they'd run out of money to make computers, shoes, movies, corn chips, bicycles, and jeans ... Your life would be vastly different without the stock market. It's the hub of our America's economy.

What do bears and bulls have to do with the stock market. These are the two most used descriptive terms used to refer to the "stock market" on any given day, or during any upswing or downswing of overall stock prices. It also refers the overall attitude of individual investors, in that one is either a bear or bull.

A bull market is a market that has been gaining value over a prolonged period. A bull market person is one with a positive or optimistic outlook for the general market, a market segment or industry, or for particular stocks (e.g., a Coca-Cola bull).

A bear market is when the overall market loses value over an extended period of time. There is no "official" definition of what makes a bear market, though many feel a drop of at least 10% is needed. A drop of something less than 10% is often called a "correction" (even though the term "correction" is never used when the market moves up 10%).

HOW IT WORKS

You might have heard of the New York Stock Exchange (NYSE). Or, you may have heard of Wall Street, which is the street in Manhattan on which the NYSE is located.

The NYSE is a wild place to visit. It might remind you of a carnival and a high school lunch cafeteria all rolled into one. People who work at the NYSE, called floor brokers, do lots of shouting and gesturing to one another as they buy and sell stocks each business day.

But the buying/selling doesn't start there. Suppose someone in Dallas Texas decides to buy stock in Uncle Fred's. The buyer contacts a local broker (which could be you) to place the order. The broker takes the buyer's money (see house accounts) and contacts a floor broker at the NYSE. Floor brokers are most often employees of a stock brokerage.

Next, the floor broker kicks into action. He or she goes to the appropriate part of the NYSE to buy Uncle Fred's stock, using what is called the open outcry system (financial term for loud scream). The floor broker sends word back to the broker that it's a done deal, and the buyer has become a stockholder.

At day's end the floor is covered with slips of paper representing bought and sold stocks. How many slips of paper? Two million exchanges--stock purchases and sales--happen on an average day of trading.

Sometime later, the stockholder may decide to sell the stock. This time the broker tells the floor broker to sell. The stockholder usually hopes to sell at a price higher than the buying price. This is not always true. There are stock sellers who hope that the price is less than when they placed there order to sell the stock. They are trading "short". "Short" is a term that means you sell stock you don't yet own at the price you can get and then later you buy the stock to meet the shares that you previously sold. If the price you paid is less that what you sold the stock for you have made a profit.

Actual trades are based on an auction market paradigm where a potential buyer bids a specific price for a stock and a potential seller asks a specific price for the stock. (Buying or selling at market means you will accept any bid or ask price for the stock.) When the bid and ask prices match, a sale takes place on a first come first serve basis if there are multiple bidders or askers at a given price.

The other type of exchange is a virtual kind, composed of a network of computers where trades are made electronically via traders at computer terminals. The best example of this is NASDAQ, which doesn't have a physical location, only a computer network.

Profit is why people buy and sell stock in the first place. Spending some money now will earn more money later--or so the stockholder hopes. It can work the other way, too. If the share price falls, the stockholder loses money when selling.

Most stocks are traded on exchanges, which are places where buyers and sellers meet and decide on a price.

DOW JONES

The Dow Jones Composite Average is a stock index that tracks 65 prominent companies. Most of the companies listed in the average trade higher or lower based on the strength of the economy, therefore they are "cyclical" companies. The average's components are every stock from the Dow Jones Industrial Average, the Dow Jones Transportation Average, and the Dow Jones Utility Average. Although the average is balanced between well-established companies (Dow Jones Industrials), transportation companies, and utility companies, the average is not widely mentioned in financial circles. Nonetheless, the average does provide a well-balanced look at the performance of the broader stock market, much like the.

OTHER EXCHANGES

Not all companies sell their stock through the NYSE. They may use some other stock exchange. All told, there are hundreds of stock exchanges around the world. In the United States, key exchanges besides the NYSE include the American Stock Exchange (AMEX) and the National Association of Securities Dealers Automated Quotations System (NASDAQ for short, pronounced "nazz-dack").

AMEX occupies a building near the NYSE. NASDAQ, however, has no physical building. With NASDAQ, buyers and sellers make their deals entirely through a computer network, rather than in face-to-face dealings. Many high-tech companies sell their stock through NASDAQ.

In addition, you'll find stock exchanges in Chicago, San Francisco, and other major U.S. cities. Other urban centers around the globe, such as London and Tokyo, also have major stock exchanges. Some people take advantage of this to trade stock 24 hours a day.

There are also systems to buy and sell lesser-priced stocks. These are the OTCBB (Over the Counter Bulletin Board) and the Pink Sheets (stocks listed on pink paper forms). Stocks that are listed OTCBB or in the Pink Sheets are sold individual to individual. Often "boiler room" brokerages offer their services to the companies who trade at this level (stock exchanges have minimum qualifications for listing) because their stock price is low, or they are a local public company.

Most stockbrokers affiliated with a brokerage do not deal often in these stocks unless they feel they are of advantage to their clients. The stocks are high risk and can offer a high return. However, the risks are so high that most sophisticated investors do not participate in these markets. Most of these stocks are only traded locally by brokers who are either not registered or who only meet the minimum requirements of the state in which they do business.

Someday we may not think of the stock market as residing on Wall Street or in any particular place. Computers and the Internet already are changing the stock market and its ancillary environment. What will the stock market of the future look like? Who knows?

Many years ago, worldwide, buyers and sellers were individual investors, such as wealthy businessmen, with long family histories (and emotional ties) to particular. Over time, markets have become more "institutionalized"; the big buyers and sellers are largely institutions (e.g., pension funds, insurance companies, mutual funds, hedge funds, investor groups, and banks).

The rise of the institutional investor has brought with it some improvements in market operations (but not necessarily in the interest of the small investor or even of the naive institutions, of which there are many). Thus, the government was responsible for "fixed" (and exorbitant) fees being markedly reduced for the 'small' investor, but only after the large institutions had managed to break the brokers' solid front on fees (they then went to 'negotiated' fees, but only for large institutions).

PRIMARY AND SECONDARY MARKETS

Primary markets (also known as capital markets) comprise of new securities to their first holders. The issue of new securities is commonly known as an Initial Public Offering (IPO). Issuers usually retain investment banks to assist them in finding buyers for these issues, and in many cases, to buy any remaining interests themselves. This arrangement is known as underwriting. In recent years the business of managing or underwriting issues of securities has been concentrated in the hands of a small number of investment banks, the most prominent of which are Goldman Sachs, Morgan Stanley and Merrill Lynch. The International Primary Markets Association (IPMA) is the trade association of banks and other investment institutions who are active in the primary markets.

In the primary markets, securities may be offered to the public in a public offer. Alternatively, they may be offered privately to a limited number of persons in a private placement. Often a combination of the two is used. The distinction between the two is important to securities regulation and company law.

Another category, sovereign debt (government bonds), is generally sold by auction to a specialized class of dealers.

Transferability is an essential characteristic of securities. This trading is called the aftermarket or secondary market. Secondary markets often consist of what is called an exchange to facilitate the meeting of buyers and sellers.

In 12th century France the *courratier de change* were concerned with managing and regulating the debts of agricultural communities on behalf of the banks. Because these men also traded with debts, they could be called the first brokers.

In late 13th century Bruges commodity traders gathered inside the house of a man called *Van der Beurse*, and in 1309 they institutionalized this until then informal meeting and became the "Brugse Beurse". The idea quickly spread around Flanders and neighbouring counties and "Beurzen" soon opened in Ghent and Amsterdam.

In the middle of the 13th century Venetian bankers began to trade in government securities. In 1351 the Venetian government outlawed spreading rumors intended to lower the price of government funds. Bankers in Pisa, Verona, Genoa and Florence also began trading in government securities during the 14th century. This was only possible because these were independent city states not ruled by a duke but a council of influential citizens.

The Dutch later started joint stock companies, which let shareholders invest in business ventures and get a share of their profits - or losses. In 1602, the Dutch East India Company issued the first shares on the Amsterdam Stock Exchange. It was the first company to issue stocks and bonds.

The Dutch also pioneered short selling, option trading, debt-equity swaps, merchant banking, unit trusts and other speculative instruments.

There are now stock markets in virtually every developed and most developing economies, with the world's biggest markets being in the United States, UK, Germany, France, and Japan.

The stock market is one of the most important sources for companies to raise money. Experience has taught us that the price of shares and other assets is an important part of the dynamics of economic growth. Rising share prices, for instance, tend to be associated with increased business investment and vice versa. Share prices also affect the wealth of households and their consumption.

The financial system in most western countries has undergone a remarkable transformation. One feature of this development is disintermediation. Unlike in history, a portion of the funds involved in saving and financing flows directly to the financial markets instead of being routed via banks' traditional lending and deposit operations.

The general public's heightened interest in investing in the stock market, either directly or through mutual funds, has been an important component of this process. Statistics show that in recent decades shares have made up an increasingly large proportion of households' financial assets in many countries.

In all developed economic systems, such as the European Union, the United States, Japan and other first world countries, the trend has been the same: Saving has moved away from traditional (government insured) bank deposits to more risky securities of one sort or another.

Today, average individuals face sometimes very difficult risk management decisions that were not required of previous generations. Both opportunities and risks for the individual investor have been amplified many times over. The average investor still lacks the relevant knowledge. Everyone cannot be a specialist in risk management and financial theory. This situation creates the opportunity environment for the stockbroker.

WHAT DOES A BROKER DO?

In order to buy shares of stock, a stockbroker may be needed to help with the transaction. In the same way that your local new car dealer is the "middleman" between you and the manufacturer, the broker (also called a stockbroker) is the link between you and a stock exchange.

To better understand what a broker is and how they operate you need to know the brokers role. A stockbroker is a salesperson. He/she works for a stock brokerage house (like Merrill Lynch or Charles Schwab). The broker's job is to carry out your transactions. Here are some common questions regarding stockbrokers:

How does a stockbroker get paid?

Salary, commissions on sales, or a mix of both is how brokers are paid.

What qualifies someone to become a stockbroker?

Stockbrokers must pass two licensing examinations called the Series 7 and Series 63. Successfully completing these exams allows the broker to advise you, to solicit business from you, and to execute transactions on your behalf.

A broker is employed by a brokerage house to facilitate client transactions and, in the case of full-service brokers, to advise you in making your investment decisions.

Although a broker may do his own research, he is NOT a research analyst. Research analysts are other folks who work for brokerages, and it is they who do that sort of enlightening, in-depth research of a company's business and industry.

TWO TYPES OF BROKERAGES

There are at least 60+ discount brokerage houses and many, many full-service brokerage houses.

The most important part of the process is determining what the client needs. Below is a general description of the services offered by full-service and discount brokers.

.

Full Service: These brokers offer a wider variety of financial products, as well as investment advice and research. They charge considerably higher fees. They may offer stocks, bonds, derivatives, annuities, and insurance. A full service broker solicits business and is paid mostly by commissions. This means that he/she is compensated not according to how well your portfolio does, but by how often you trade. This in turn means that it is in his/her interest to have you trade as often as possible. This is one reason that some people eschew full service brokers.

Discount Brokers: Discount brokerages do not offer any advice or research. They simply transact customer's trades with no frills. Because they manage fewer products than their full-service counterparts, discounters charge considerably lower fees. They also often offer online computer order entry services. Live brokers at these brokerages are usually paid a fixed salary to execute your trades. They don't solicit, and they aren't paid commissions. Discount brokerages make money by doing business in volume, competing mostly on price and "reliability" of the service: if they have the lowest prices and the best service, they get the most trades.

Online Trading

Online trading has exploded over the past few years, as investors are becoming more self-sufficient and comfortable using their computers for investing. Many discount brokers offer both options and, in general, the price of transacting a trade with a real live human being will be somewhat higher than if you conduct it on the Internet.

Online brokerage accounts are becoming easier to use and are providing more and more information, but you need to know how you can access your account information if you can't get online for some reason and need to make a transaction. Will a "live" broker be accessible to you if you need to place a trade? What if you need a copy of your latest monthly statements for the IRS and the web site is down?

Placing an Order

You buy a stock because you think it's a great long-term prospect, and you only sell it when you either need the money or feel that there's a better place to put that money. There are different types of orders and they are:

Buy order: The order placed when shares are purchased. There are several types of buy orders.

Buy at market: The broker is instructed to buy a specified number of shares at the prevailing market price.

Buy at a limit: The broker is instructed to buy a specified number of shares, but only at a specified price or lower.

Sell order: An order placed to sell shares.

Sell at market: An order to sell shares at the prevailing market price.

Sell at a limit: An order to sell shares only at the price that you specify or higher.

Sell at a stop limit: The broker is instructed to sell the stock if it falls to a certain price.

TYPES OF SECURITIES

Originally the term "securities" was used to denote security interests (such as mortgages and charges) supporting the payment of a debt or other obligation. In Early modern Europe, companies and government agencies began to raise capital from the public using secured debt obligations, which came to be known as "securities". As shares became more readily transferable from the Victorian era, their functional similarity to debt securities became clearer, and both forms of investment became known as "securities". More recently, the term has also been extended to include units in investment funds and other forms of readily transferable investment.

The concept of "securities" should be distinguished from "interests in securities". The latter are the assets of a client from whom an intermediary holds securities on an unallocated basis, commingled with the interests in securities of other clients. The distinction between securities and interests in securities is often overlooked in practice.

USE OF SECURITIES

For the issuer:

Issuers of securities include commercial companies, government agencies, local authorities and international and supranational organizations (such as the World Bank). Debt securities issued by the government (called government bonds or sovereign bonds) generally carry a lower interest rate than corporate debt issued by commercial companies. Repackaged securities are usually issued by a company established for the purpose of the repackaging - called a special purpose vehicle (SPV).

New capital: Commercial enterprises have traditionally used securities as a means of raising new capital. Securities are an attractive option relative to bank loans, which tend to be relatively expensive and short term. Another disadvantage of bank loans as a source of financing is that the bank may seek a measure of control over the business of the borrower via financial covenants. Through securities, capital is provided by investors who purchase the securities.

Repackaging: In recent decades securities have been issued to repackage existing assets. In a traditional securitization, a financial institution may wish to remove assets from its balance sheet in order to achieve regulatory capital efficiencies or to accelerate its receipt of cash flow from the original assets. Alternatively, an intermediary may wish to make a profit by acquiring financial assets and repackaging them in a way which makes them more attractive to investors.

For the holder:

Investors in securities may be retail, i.e. members of the public investing other than by way of business. Retail is sole purview of the stockbroker. The greatest volume of investment is done wholesale, i.e. by financial institutions acting on their own account, or on behalf of clients. Important institutional investors include investment banks, insurance companies, pension funds and other managed funds.

Investment: The traditional economic function of the purchase of securities is investment, with the view to receiving income and/or achieving capital gain.

Debt securities generally offer a higher rate of interest than bank deposits, and equities may offer the prospect of capital growth. Equity investment may also offer control of the business of the issuer. Debt holdings may also offer some measure of control to the investor if the company is a fledgling start-up or an old giant undergoing 'restructuring'. In these cases, if interest payments are missed, the creditors may take control of the company and liquidate it to recover some of their investment.

Securities are traditionally divided into debt securities and equities.

Debt:

The holder of a debt security, typically a bond, is owed a debt by the issuer and is entitled to the payment of principal and interest, together with other personal rights under the terms of the issue, such as the right to receive certain information. Debt securities are generally issued for a fixed term and redeemable by the issuer at the end of that term.

Government bonds: These are medium or long term debt securities issued by sovereign governments or their agencies. Typically they carry a lower rate of interest than corporate bonds. In addition to serving as a source of finance for governments, treasuries are used to manage the money supply in the money market operations of central banks.

Money market instruments: These are short term debt instruments, such as certificates of deposit, commercial paper and certain bills of exchange. They are highly liquid and are sometimes referred to as "near cash".

Euro securities: These are securities issued internationally outside their domestic market. They include eurobonds and euronotes. Eurobonds are characteristically underwritten, and not secured, and interest is paid gross. A euro note may take the form of euro-commercial paper (ECP) or euro-certificates of deposit.

Equity:

The holder of an equity is a shareholder. A share of stock is the smallest unit of ownership in a company. If you own a share of a company's stock, you are a part owner of the company.

You have the right to vote on members of the board of directors and other important matters before the company. If the company distributes profits to shareholders, you will likely receive a proportionate share.

One of the unique features of stock ownership is the notion of limited liability. If the company loses a lawsuit and must pay a huge judgment, the worse that can happen is your stock becomes worthless. The creditors can't come after your personal assets, which isn't necessarily true in privately held companies. There are two types of stock:

Common stock

Common stock represents the majority of stock held by the public. It has voting rights, along with the right to share in dividends.

When you hear or read about "stocks" being up or down, it always refers to common stock. Most of the stock held by individuals is common stock.

Preferred stock

Despite its name, preferred stock has fewer rights than common stock, except in one important area – dividends. Companies that issue preferred stocks usually pay consistent dividends and preferred stock has first call on dividends over common stock. Investors buy preferred stock for its current income from dividends, so look for companies that make big profits to use preferred stock to return some of those profits via dividends.

Some companies will issue two classes of stock when they go public. Class A shares go to the public as common stock, which carry one vote per share. The company founders may issue themselves class B stock, which has 10 votes per share, thus guaranteeing that they will retain control of the company.

The class of stock is often used to refer to groups of stocks. In this case the class of stock is a descriptive term, as below:

Blue-chip stocks: These include the most prestigious well-established large companies. Many of these are household names such as Disney, IBM or Coca-Cola. These are typically older companies that the public has come to know and trust. They are also often included in the Dow Jones Average.

Growth stocks: As the name might suggest, these stocks have strong growth potential. These are typically companies that are newer, doing research and developing products and services in hopes of achieving growth. Much of the profits are fed back into the companies themselves.

Value stocks: These are stocks in companies that, for one of many reasons, are undervalued. They are stocks that are selling at a low price, but when analyzing the company's sales, earnings and looking at other factors, give indications that they should be selling for a higher per share price.

Cyclical stocks: The earnings on these stocks are tied very closely to the overall business cycle and economic state. Examples include the housing industry and industrial equipment companies.

Defensive stocks: These remain stable in any economic conditions, such as food companies, drug manufacturers or utilities. These are stocks in companies that manufacture the necessities that people will need in any economy.

Income stocks: These pay higher-than-average dividends over a sustained period. They are typically long-established companies with stable earnings or utilities such as phone companies and power companies.

Speculative stocks: These are stocks in emerging companies that are speculating on their future earnings and revenue. These are risky investments since the company may or may not reach their intended future goals.

Hybrids

Hybrid securities combine some of the characteristics of both debt and equity securities.

Preference shares: These shares form an intermediate class of security between equities and debt. If the issuer is liquidated, they carry the right to receive interest and/or a return of capital in priority to ordinary shareholders.

Convertibles: These are bonds that can be converted, at the election of the bondholder, into another sort of security such as equities.

Equity warrants: These are contractual entitlements to purchase shares on pre-determined terms. They are often issued together with bonds or existing equities, but are detachable from them and separately tradable.

OTHER METHODS OF OWNING OR CONTROLLING SHARES

One doesn't necessarily have to own shares in a company to participate in their stock. There are other possibilities, such as:

Call option

An option contract that grants the buyer the right, but not the obligation, to buy the optioned shares of a company at a set price (called the "strike price") for a certain period of time. If the stock fails to meet the strike price before the expiration date, the option expires worthless. You buy a call option if you think the share price of the underlying security will rise, or sell a call option if you think it will fall. Selling an option is also referred to as "writing" an option. The option seller is called the writer.

Futures/futures contracts

This security is a contract to buy or sell an amount of a commodity for a specific price at a specific point in the future.

Naked options

These are options that are sold on securities when the seller does not actually own shares of the underlying securities -- a highly risky endeavor. Naked options are also referred to as "uncovered options."

Penny stock

A very cheap, speculative stock, selling for less than $1 a share, though the term is sometimes applied to stocks selling for up to $5 a share.

Put

A put option is a contract that gives the buyer the right, but not the obligation, to sell the stock underlying the contract at a predetermined price (the strike price). The seller (or writer) of the put option is obligated to buy the stock at the strike price. Put options can be exercised at any time before the option expires. Buy a put if you think the share price of the underlying stock will fall, or sell one if you think it will rise. The stock doesn't need to be owned to buy a put. You can buy a put, wait for the price to fall below the strike price, then buy the stock and immediately resell it for the higher strike price. The person who sold the put gets stuck with buying the stock at the higher price.

Real estate investment trust (REIT)

REITs are a specialized form of equity that allows investors to own a portion of a group of real estate properties, although many investors think of them as an alternative to bonds. Granted special tax status by the Internal Revenue Service, REITs pay out at least 95% of their earnings in the form of dividends to shareholders, often offering healthy dividend yields of the same magnitude as bonds. Even better, as REITs acquire more property and increase the value of the properties they own, the value of the equity may increase as well, providing a nice total return.

Unit investment trust (UIT)

An investment usually sold by brokers that purchases a fixed, unmanaged portfolio of stocks or other securities, and then sells shares in the trust to investors, usually in units of at least $1,000. Because they are unmanaged, unit investment trusts are somewhat like index funds. However, UITs typically have much higher sales loads and/or annual management fees, so they do not share the low-cost advantage of index funds.

Warrant

A warrant is the entitlement to purchase a certain number of shares of a particular stock at a predetermined price (usually higher than the current price) for an extended period of time. Typically, warrants are offered with a bond issue or an IPO. An example of a warrant might be the opportunity for an investor to buy 500 shares of ABC Company for $50 until September 1, 2010. Although the warrant accompanies a bond or actual IPO shares, it trades separately after it is issued.

MUTUAL FUNDS

Over the past decade, American investors increasingly have turned to mutual funds to save for retirement and other financial goals. Mutual funds can offer the advantages of diversification and professional management. But, as with other investment choices, investing in mutual funds involves risk. And fees and taxes will diminish a fund's returns.

A mutual fund is a company that pools money from many investors and invests the money in stocks, bonds, short-term money-market instruments, other securities or assets, or some combination of these investments. The combined holdings the mutual fund owns are known as its portfolio. Each share represents an investor's proportionate ownership of the fund's holdings and the income those holdings generate.

Investors purchase mutual fund shares from the fund itself (or through a broker for the fund) instead of from other investors on a secondary market, such as the New York Stock Exchange or NASDAQ.

The price that investors pay for mutual fund shares is the funds per share net asset value (NAV) plus any shareholder fees that the fund imposes at the time of purchase (such as sales loads).

Mutual fund shares are "redeemable," meaning investors can sell their shares back to the fund (or to a broker acting for the fund).

Mutual funds generally create and sell new shares to accommodate new investors. In other words, they sell their shares on a continuous basis, although some funds stop selling when, for example, they become too large.

The investment portfolios of mutual funds typically are managed by separate entities known as "investment advisers" that are registered with the SEC.

The investment portfolios of mutual funds typically are managed by separate entities known as "investment advisers" that are registered with the SEC.

DIFFERENT TYPES OF FUNDS

Most mutual funds fall into one of three main categories — money market funds, bond funds (also called "fixed income" funds), and stock funds (also called "equity" funds). Each type has different features and different risks and rewards. Generally, the higher the potential return, the higher the risk of loss.

Money Market Funds

Money market funds have relatively low risks, compared to other mutual funds (and most other investments). By law, they can invest in only certain high-quality, short-term investments issued by the U.S. government, U.S. corporations, and state and local governments. Money market funds try to keep their net asset value (NAV) — which represents the value of one share in a fund — at a stable $1.00 per share. But the NAV may fall below $1.00 if the fund's investments perform poorly. Investor losses have been rare, but they are possible.

Money market funds pay dividends that generally reflect short-term interest rates, and historically the returns for money market funds have been lower than for either bond or stock funds. That's why "inflation risk" — the risk that inflation will outpace and erode investment returns over time — can be a potential concern for investors in money market funds.

Bond Funds

Bond funds generally have higher risks than money market funds, largely because they typically pursue strategies aimed at producing higher yields. Unlike money market funds, the SEC's rules do not restrict bond funds to high-quality or short-term investments. Because there are many different types of bonds, bond funds can vary dramatically in their risks and rewards.

Some of the risks associated with bond funds include:

Credit Risk: The possibility that company or other issuers whose bonds are owned by the fund may fail to pay their debts (including the debt owed to holders of their bonds). Credit risk is less of a factor for bond funds that invest in insured bonds or U.S. Treasury bonds. By contrast, those that invest in the bonds of companies with poor credit ratings generally will be subject to higher risk.

Interest Rate Risk: The risk that the market value of the bonds will go down when interest rates go up. Because of this, you can lose money in any bond fund, including those that invest only in insured bonds or Treasury bonds. Funds that invest in longer-term bonds tend to have higher interest rate risk.

Prepayment Risk: The chance that a bond will be paid off early. For example, if interest rates fall, a bond issuer may decide to pay off (or "retire") its debt and issue new bonds that pay a lower rate. When this happens, the fund may not be able to reinvest the proceeds in an investment with as high a return or yield.

Stock Funds

Although a stock fund's value can rise and fall quickly (and dramatically) over the short term, historically stocks have performed better over the long term than other types of investments — including corporate bonds, government bonds, and treasury securities. Overall "market risk" poses the greatest potential danger for investors in stocks funds. Stock prices can fluctuate for a broad range of reasons — such as the overall strength of the economy or demand for particular products or services.

Not all stock funds are the same. For example:

Growth funds focus on stocks that may not pay a regular dividend but have the potential for large capital gains.

Income funds invest in stocks that pay regular dividends.

Index funds aim to achieve the same return as a particular market index, such as the S&P 500 Composite Stock Price Index, by investing in all — or perhaps a representative sample — of the companies included in an index.

Sector funds may specialize in a particular industry segment, such as technology or consumer products stocks.

CLASSES OF FUNDS

Many mutual funds offer more than one class of shares. For example, you may have seen a fund that offers "Class A" and "Class B" shares. Each class will invest in the same "pool" (or investment portfolio) of securities and will have the same investment objectives and policies. But each class will have different shareholder services and/or distribution arrangements with different fees and expenses. As a result, each class will likely have different performance results.

A multi-class structure offers investors the ability to select a fee and expense structure that is most appropriate for their investment goals (including the time that they expect to remain invested in the fund). Here are some key characteristics of the most common mutual fund share classes offered to individual investors:

Class A Shares: These shares typically impose a front-end sales load. They also tend to have lower annual expenses than other mutual fund share classes. Be aware that some mutual funds reduce the front-end load as the size of your investment increases.

Class B Shares: These shares typically do not have a front-end sales load. Instead, they may impose a contingent deferred sales load and a \ fee (along with other annual expenses). Class B shares also might convert automatically to a class with a lower 12b-1 fee if the investor holds the shares long enough.

Class C Shares: These shares might have a 12b-1 fee, other annual expenses, and either a front- or back-end sales load. But the front- or back-end load for Class C shares tends to be lower than for Class A or Class B shares, respectively. Unlike Class B shares, Class C shares generally do not convert to another class. Class C shares tend to have higher annual expenses than either Class A or Class B shares.

There are three key things to know about mutual funds:

Mutual funds are not guaranteed or insured by the FDIC or any other government agency — even if you buy through a bank and the fund carries the bank's name. You can lose money investing in mutual funds.

Past performance is not a reliable indicator of future performance. So don't be dazzled by last year's high returns. But past performance can help you assess a fund's volatility over time.

All mutual funds have costs that lower your investment returns. One example is the back end load, which is a pernicious and usually not fully explained sales fee charged by some mutual funds when an investor sells fund shares. Also called a contingent deferred sales charge. Another example is the front-end load, where fees are charged when the buy-in to the fund occurs. These fees are generally 5% of amount invested.

The shareholders through what is called a 12b-1 fee often pay mutual fund promotional expenses such as advertising and public relations.

HEDGE FUNDS

"Hedge fund" is a general, non-legal term used to describe private, unregistered investment pools that traditionally have been limited to sophisticated, wealthy investors. Hedge funds are *not* mutual funds and, as such, are *not* subject to the numerous regulations that apply to mutual funds for the protection of investors — including regulations requiring a certain degree of liquidity, regulations requiring that mutual fund shares be redeemable at any time, regulations protecting against conflicts of interest, regulations to assure fairness in the pricing of fund shares, disclosure regulations, regulations limiting the use of leverage, and more.

"Funds of hedge funds," a relatively new type of investment product, are investment companies that invest in hedge funds. Some, but not all, register with the SEC and file semi-annual reports. They often have lower minimum investment thresholds than traditional, unregistered hedge funds and can sell their shares to a larger number of investors. Like hedge funds, funds of hedge funds are not mutual funds. Unlike open-end mutual funds, funds of hedge funds offer very limited rights of redemption.

BEARER SECURITIES

Bearer securities are issued in the form of a paper instrument. On the face of the instrument is written the promise of the issuer to pay the bearer of the instrument. By a legal fiction, the instrument is deemed to constitute the debt of the issuer, and not merely to represent them. In the absence of computerization, bearer securities constitute tangible assets/ They are transferred by delivering the instrument from person to person. In some cases, transfer is by endorsement, or signing the back of the instrument, and delivery.

Regulatory and fiscal authorities sometimes regard bearer securities negatively, as they may be used to facilitate the evasion of regulatory restrictions and tax.

REGISTERED SECURITIES

In the case of registered securities, certificates bearing the name of the holder are issued, but these merely represent the securities. A person does not automatically acquire legal ownership by having possession of the certificate. The issuer maintains a register (usually maintained by an appointed registrar) in which details of the holder of the securities are entered and updated as appropriate. Unlike bearer securities, registered securities comprise of a bundle of intangible rights including the right of the shareholder to share in all the assets of a company, subject to all the liabilities of the company. A transfer of registered securities is effected by amending the register.

Traditionally, the delivery of bearer instruments by way of pledge has been widely used in the securities markets to collaterize financial exposures. The delivery of certificates to registered securities has also been widely used in collateral arrangements. However, because registered securities are not tangible assets, the legal effect of such a delivery is generally characterized not as pledge, but rather equitable mortgage.

DIVIDED AND UNDIVIDED SECURITIES

The terms "divided" and "undivided" relate to the proprietary nature of a security.

Each divided security constitutes a separate asset, which is legally distinct from each other security in the same issue. Pre-electronic bearer securities were divided. Each instrument constitutes the separate covenant of the issuer and is a separate debt.

With undivided securities, the entire issue makes up one single asset, with each of the securities being a fractional part of this undivided whole. Shares in the secondary markets are always undivided. The issuer owes only one set of obligations to shareholders under its memorandum, articles of association and company law. A share represents an undivided fractional part of the issuing company. Registered debt securities also have this undivided nature.

FUNGIBLE AND NON-FUNGIBLE SECURITIES

The terms "fungible" and "non-fungible" relate to the way in which securities are held.

If an asset is fungible, this means that when such an asset is lent, or placed with a custodian, it is customary for the borrower or custodian to be obliged at the end of the loan or custody arrangement to return assets equivalent to the original asset, rather than the identical asset. In other words, the redelivery of fungibles is equivalent and not *in specie* (identical).

Undivided securities are always fungible by logical necessity. Divided securities may or may not be fungible, depending on market practice. The clear trend is towards fungible arrangements.

THE REGULATORS, THE SECURITIES AND EXCHANGE COMMISSION

The mission of the U.S. Securities and Exchange Commission (SEC) is to protect investors, maintain fair, orderly, and efficient markets, and facilitate capital formation. Although last in priority capital formation is a key element in the economy of the United States. As population growth, inward migration (legal and illegal), burgeoning technological growth act on society the need for new money increases exponentially.

The laws and rules that govern the securities industry in the United States derive from a simple and straightforward concept: all investors, whether large institutions or private individuals, should have access to certain basic facts about an investment prior to buying it, and so long as they hold it. The SEC requires public companies to disclose meaningful and significant financial and other information to the public. This creates a common pool of knowledge for all investors to use to determine whether to buy, sell, or hold a particular security.

The SEC oversees securities exchanges, securities brokers and dealers, investment advisors, and mutual funds. The SEC is concerned primarily with promoting the disclosure of important market-related information, maintaining fair dealing, and protecting against fraud.

Each year the SEC initiates hundreds of civil enforcement actions against individuals and companies for securities laws violations. The most frequent infractions include insider trading, accounting fraud, and providing false or misleading information about securities and the companies that issue them.

BRIEF HISTORY OF THE SEC

Based on Congressional findings in hearings into the Great Crash of 29', Congress passed the Securities Act of 1933 and the Securities Exchange Act of 1934. These laws were designed to restore investor confidence in American capital markets by providing more structure and government oversight. The laws had two main purposes:

> Companies publicly offering securities for investment dollars must tell the public the truth about their businesses, the securities they are selling, and the risks involved in investing.

> People who sell and trade securities – brokers, dealers, and exchanges – must treat investors fairly and honestly, putting investors' interests first.

Monitoring the securities industry requires a highly coordinated effort. Congress established the Securities and Exchange Commission in 1934 to enforce the newly passed securities laws, to promote stability in the markets and, most importantly, to protect investors. President Franklin Delano Roosevelt appointed Joseph P. Kennedy, President John F. Kennedy's father, to serve as the first Chairman of the SEC.

HOW TO BECOME A STOCKBROKER

If you have an interest in becoming a stockbroker the first thing you should be absolutely sure of is that you have the dedication to make a go of it. Being a stockbroker can be fast paced and rewarding, but you must be willing to take the risk and put yourself forward to make it happen in a positive way for your and your clients.

Oddly enough just about anyone can be a broker. It doesn't require any level of education or experience. In other words you don't need a college degree, or even a high school graduate for that matter. But that doesn't mean you don't have to have the right knowledge and personality to become a success at it. In fact most brokers are college graduates with degrees in finance, economics, or business.

The thing you must do to become a stockbroker is pass the General Securities Registered Representative Examination (Series 7 exam), administered by the National Association of Securities Dealers (NASD). Most states also require the Uniform Securities Agents State Law Examination (Series 63 exam) and the Uniform Investment Advisor Law Exam (Series 65 exam) as well.

One you have passed and hold these licenses, you cannot just begin to buy and sell stock because you don't have a connection to an exchange to "execute" your trades. A trade is any stock transaction, buy or sell. You need to be affiliated with a stock brokerage with a "seat" on an exchange to accomplish trades.

Having a seat means that the firm has a trading license issued by the Exchange is required to effect transactions on the floor of the Exchange or through any facility thereof. Only qualified and approved member organizations may acquire and hold a trading license. Trading Licenses are available for $54,219 per year and billed monthly, pro-rated for the amount of time remaining for the year. The maximum number of Trading Licenses available is 1,366.

One way to affiliate is to take advantage of on the job training offered by most brokerage firms. This training prepares you to take the exams. This preparation can be a process taking from four to six months. The exams are not the type that you can just walk in off the street and take and expect to pass. You must retain a significant amount of knowledge to pass the exams. When you pass the required exams you will become a registered representative of your sponsoring firm (brokerage).

Another way, although much more difficult, is to start trading in your own state and stay under $25 million total in managed accounts of your clients. Your trades still need to be executed by a brokerage with a "seat" on an exchange. In this case your relationship to the broker is the same as a client, only you pay a greatly reduced commission to execute the trades of your clients. You will also likely buy and sell more stocks listed no the OTCBB and in pink sheets that those listed on the NYSE, AMEX, or NASDAQ.

Once you have the requisite experience you can take the master broker test and become licensed as your own stock brokerage. Keep in mind however, that while a stockbroker is responsible to his/her clients, a master broker or principle broker also has significant fiduciary responsibilities as well.

WHAT'S EXPECTED FROM A STOCKBROKER

It is important that you understand what your customers, employers and peers will expect of you in terms of performance and conformity. All types of brokers must obtain and maintain their licensing to function professionally and legally. From their the type of broker you choose to be dictates the remaining elements in your job description.

If your are full service broker, you should completely understand the fact that your first priority is to generate buying and selling in a community of clients that you alone are responsible for soliciting, servicing, and monitoring. Your best client will be the one with the most trades and transactions.

The reason is that this is what pays you! If you're on salary the revenue you generate in commissions for the "house" (brokerage) is what pays that salary. If you're on commission, then those fees represent your only income from the job.

You must have excellent people skills as well as a very high level of sales ability to be a success as a full service stockbroker. You are competing with self-service companies that charge significantly less than you do. Your credibility and integrity are your main personal selling points.

You must have current and even premonitionary knowledge of a wide variety of stocks, bonds, mutual funds, money funds, stock funds, and a myriad of other financial instruments and securities (See Types of Securities). Or specialize in certain areas of the marketplace. You will have research support to provide you with ammunition.

In either case you will need to keep your clients aware of changes, opportunities, etc., in order to generate buy and sell orders. Clients who buy a "portfolio" and then sit on it for years are not the type of client you would consider as a good client. Again, your job is generate revenue and the only way you can do that is sell you clients on new buys and new sells on a regular basis.

History tells us that from the inception of the SEC and the regulated stock market (1935) until the rise of the Internet, the only access the public had to buy and sell securities and bonds was through a full service broker.

The Internet and its rapid installation as a basic business, finance, and communication platform for an entire society has wrought new types of stockbrokers.

If you become a discount broker the major difference between you and full service broker is that you will not individual solicit any clients. You will be paid a salary to execute trades that come to you through your company's presence on the Internet (web site). The portfolio of instruments that you sell will also be much smaller. And, you are not responsible for the investment strategies of your customers. Your only responsibility is to execute their trades successfully. Your company, and you, will prosper only if you provide good consistent service at a very competitive (cheap) price.

CHEAPER ISN'T ALWAYS BETTER

It may surprise to know that cheaper isn't always better for everyone. The price per trade at a discount broker may also indicate the level of customer service that comes with it. Investors know that. Some want to be serviced and some want to be do-it-yourselfers, and some want to be day traders. Each has their own set of factors in considering their full service broker or discount broker.

CUSTOMER SERVICE IS THE KEY

If nothing else any investor will do is research the customer service that a brokerage provides. In the case of a discount broker the web site is the key element. The web site must be easy to navigate and it must also have the ability to initiate voice communication through the site and over the telephone. Keep in mind the investor who uses the Internet can quickly find out how your brokerage is rated for customer service.

HOW BROKERS ARE EVALUATED BY CLIENTELE

If you are thinking of becoming a broker, or if you are ready to open your first discount brokerage account, or if you are looking to work with a full service broker, or if you are wondering if you're getting the best service for your money from your current one, here are the ten things that you or your clientele will use to make your evaluation:

1. Trading Commissions

Cheaper is not always better. You have probably figured that out, but the price per trade at a discount broker may also indicate the level of customer service that comes with it. If you aren't trading in and out of stocks very often and you're not too concerned about whether your trade is executed within 15 seconds or 2 minutes there really isn't a significant difference among the brokers charging $7 to $20. Any cheaper than that and you may have trouble getting someone on the telephone to answer any questions you may have. And in reverse if you are paying much more than that, your service had better be perfect.

2. Other fees

Beyond the trading commissions, brokerages may charge other fees, including fees for transferring assets into the account, fees for closing an account, IRA custodian fees, wire transfer fees, account inactivity fees, annual fees, and fees for not maintaining a minimum balance.

3. Minimum initial deposit

Investors should know what amount they wish to invest. Brokers may have minimum account requirements.

4. Customer service

This is a consequential part of the formula now matter how the service is delivered. Full service broker should be totally involved in a complete customer service program. Discount brokers should be totally involved in delivering online service and support that is easy to access, easy to use, and emotes comfort and security. The ability to also communicate with discount brokers via telephone is also critical.

5. Traditional banking services

This might not be tops on your list, and we haven't broached the subject, but people do think about looking for a brokerage account that can accommodate their banking needs. As a result, many brokers now offer: Money market sweeps; Check writing and bill payment; Visa cards; Direct deposit; And, ATM cards

6. Research

All types of brokers use market research as a marketing tool and some brokerages market their research as a real plus. It shouldn't be a surprise that most people do not want to pay for research as a separate item.

7. Mutual funds

No-load mutual funds can be purchased directly from mutual fund companies and therefore generally has no impact on broker evaluation. No-load mutual funds can be purchased from discount brokers and should be without paying a transaction fee. Typically discount brokers only offer a small part of the funds available in the market.

8. Investment product selection

All the brokerages offer stocks traded on the major exchanges, and most will offer equity mutual funds. But there are a number of other investment vehicles that clients may wish to use. The high risk over the counter market is popular with some who like to gamble and some brokerages accommodate.

9. Other methods of getting your trades executed

What if the Internet breaks? Investors check out whether the brokerages they're considering also have touch-tone phone trading, and how that works. Sometimes they just might want to place an order through a real, live person, and many discount brokerages offer that option, too.

10. Other freebies and perks

The investors know that these are only one-time things usually and therefore not a major factor in their decisions. However, free money is free money and could be a determining factor.

If an investor is only making five, six, ten, even twenty trades in a year, the difference between paying $7.00 per trade and $20.00 per trade isn't significant. Customer service is the priority.

OUTLOOK FOR STOCKBROKERS AND BROKERAGES

America has become a society of equity investors. The number of household owning equities has increased more than three-fold since the early 1980s. Half of the approximately fifty seven million United States households own stocks directly or through mutual funds. The number of households holding equities since 1999 has increased 7.1 million and by 2.8 million since 2002, according the Investment Company Institute and the Securities Industry Association. The majority of the growth has come from the increased availability of defined contribution retirement plans, particularly 401k plans, where the majority of investments are made in stock funds.

The growth from the 1980s has been three fold, compared to increase in the number of households in the United States of 35%.

This growth in household equity ownership has been consistent through both bull and bear markets. And survived the great contraction of the markets in 2000 to 2002. However the growth rate of equity ownership ha slowed considerably since the 1990s.

Several factors seem to have contributed to the slowdown. The growth in the number of workers enrolled in defined contribution plans has decreased. This is due to the late 1990s most large employers had instituted such plans. Since the mid 1990s growth has come from small businesses that have fewer workers.

The value of investment portfolios has increased to a median household level in 2005 of $65,000, compared with $50,000 in 1999.

Equity ownership once on the purview of the rich and sophisticated has spread to a broad cross section of demographic groups. Younger owners tend to hold equities in mutual funds and in tax-deferred account and are more likely to have first invested through a work related retirement plan. Older investors are more like to have purchased their first equity investments outside of these plans.

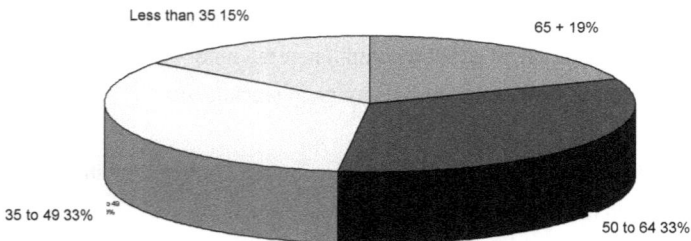

Less than 35 15%   65 + 19%

35 to 49 33%   50 to 64 33%

Nearly all equity owners in 2005 follow a buy-and-hold investment philosophy (ICI & SIA Study) and view their equity holdings as long term investments. They are also less like to take substantial or above average financial risk with their stocks or mutual funds.

Equity investors tend to be middle-aged, with moderate household incomes and financial assets. According to the ICI & SIA Study the following are the characteristics of equity investors:

How many Americans own equities?

Individuals	91.1 million
Households	56.9 million

Who are they?

Median age	51 years
Median household income	$65,000
Married or living with partner	70%
College graduates	56%
Employed	70%
Retired	29%
Saving for retirement	88%

What do they own?

Median household financial assets	$125,000
Median percent of financial assets in equities	55%
IRA account ownership	
67%	
Participate in retirement plan	78%

What is in their equity portfolios?

Own stock mutual funds	90%
Own individual stock	
49%	

Does age and education make a difference?

Age	Median $ Equity	Median %
Less than 35	$33,800	
59		
35 to 49 years	$50,200	
59		
50 to 64 years	$87,500	
54		
65 years or older	$103,800	
41		
HS graduate or less	$40,000	50
Some college or Assoc. deg.	$50,000	53
College or post grad deg.	$78,000	57

Age plays a vital role in investors and the goals. The chart below shows the variances.

VARIANCE BY AGE OF INVESTOR'S FINANCIAL GOALS

	All Equity Investors	Less than 35 Years	35 to 49 Years	50 to 64 Years	65 Years Or Older
FINANCIAL GOALS					
Retirement	88	93	93	92	69
Inheritance	49	51	42	45	64
Emergency	56	62	53	56	58
Minimize taxes	51	47	53	56	45
Education	31	55	48	16	9
Current Income	32	22	19	31	63
Large Purchase	17	34	21	11	6
PRIMARY FINANCIAL GOALS					
Retirement	60	55	65	73	32
Education	9	17	15	3	1
Current Income	10	3	3	9	32
Emergency	6	7	4	5	8
Minimize taxes	4	1	4	3	6
Inheritance	7	6	4	4	18
Large Purchase	3	8	4	2	1
Other	1	3	1	1	2

Investors are more diversified in 2005. More investors own foreign equity holdings primarily through global stock funds. More investors own hybrid mutual funds, annuities, investment real estate, individual bonds, and bond mutual funds.

Nearly three quarters of all equity investors hold equities outside of retirement plans. More than three quarters of investors who hold equities outside employer-sponsored plans purchased equities through advisers. The largest segment us advisers as their sole means for purchasing equities.

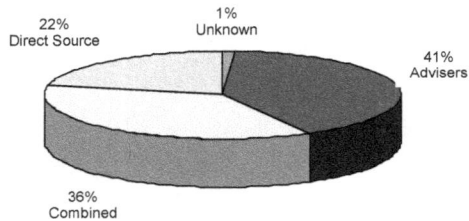

Equity investors reported use of professionals includes either financial advisers or stockbrokers. Thirty nine percent use full service brokers, twenty eight percent use financial planners, and ten percent use bank or savings institutions as advisers.

Percentage of Ownership through Brokers

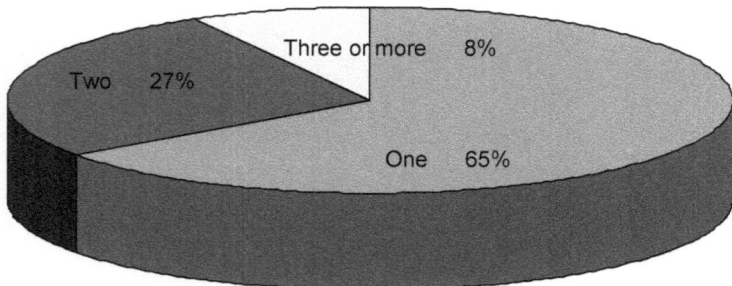

The rise of the Internet has obviously spawned a whole new segment in the financial markets, the discount broker. Consequently investors can now trade their equities via the Internet. As the following graphic shows, all types of investors use the Internet.

INTERNET USAGE 2005

	Used the Internet For A Financial Related Purpose	Did Not Use The Internet For A Financial Related Purpose
Age of Investor		
Less than 35	77	23
35 to 49	72	28
50 to 64	69	31
65 or older	47	53
Decision Maker in the Household		
Male	73	27
Female	55	45
Co-decision makers	70	30
Education		
High school or less	41	59
Some college Assoc. Deg.	64	36
College or post grad. Deg.	77	23
Household Income		
Less than $50,000	48	52
$50,000 to $99,999	72	28
$100,000 to $149,000	81	19
$150,000 or more	91	9

MOST EQUITY INVESTORS USE THE INTERNET FOR SOME TYPE OF FINANCIAL TRANSACTION.

MOST EQUITY INVESTORS USE THE INTERNET

	Percent
Any financial related use	68
Type o Financial relatd use	
Accessed financial accounts	50
Obtained financial news	46
Collected retirement information	29
Sent an email to broker or adviser	20
Conducted an equity transaction	14

EQUITY INVESTORS AND DIVERSIFICATION

Equity investors as a whole do not trade very often. They have since 1999 diversified in to more types of financial instruments.

INCREASED OWNERSHIP OF VARIOUS TYPES OF SECURITIES

	1999	2002	2005
Saving accounts, money markets			
or certificates of deposit	83	86	83
Hybrid mutual funds	39	52	62
Money market mutual funds	26	35	42
Investment real estate	26	24	30
Fixed or variable annuities	21	23	28
Bond Investments (total)	22	36	38
Individual Bonds (excluding US Savings bonds)	9	17	16
Bond mutual funds	16	26	31
US Savings Bonds	n/a	n/a	37
Exchanged-traded funds	n/a	n/a	3

HOW OFTEN DO EQUITY INVESTORS TRADE

Most investors who own equities execute only a small number of transactions in any given year. The following chart illustrates this point:

EQUITY INVESTORS BY TRANSACTION ACTIVITY

	1998	2001	2004
Conducted equity transactions	42	40	40
Bought equities	39	31	32
Sold equities	27	24	27
Did not conduct equity transactions	58	60	60

HOLDINGS OUTSIDE OF EMPLOYER RETIREMENT PLANS

INDIVIDUAL STOCK OUTSIDE EMPLOYER-SPONSORED RETIREMENT BY %

	1999	2002	2005
Individual Stock Assets Held	9	5	4
Less than $1000	13	16	12
$1000 to $4999	10	10	11
$5000 to $9999	19	22	20
$10000 to $29999	23	20	24
$30000 to $99999	9	11	10
$100000 to $199999	9	7	10
$200000 to $499999	9	7	10
$500000 to $999999	4	5	5
$1 million or more	4	4	4
Mean	$172,900	$157,500	$199,400
Median	$25,000	$25,000	$35,000

	1999	2002	2005
Number of stocks owned			
1	27	22	25
2	17	17	13
3 to 5	26	25	25
6 to 9	11	13	14
10 to 19	12	14	12
20 or more	7	9	11
Mean	6	7	8
Median	3	4	4
Length of ownership			
2 years or less	13	12	6
3 to 5 years	15	18	21
6 to 10 years	18	18	21
11 to 15 years	14	13	13
16 to 20 years	12	10	10
21 to 30 years	12	13	16
More than 30 years	16	16	20
Mean	16 years	15 years	18 years
Median	12 years	12 years	15 years

CONCLUSION

From the information provided it is clear that the market is quite strong and there is no end to the investors seeking either full service brokerage or discount brokerage. If you are considering a career as a stockbroker, understanding this information will provide you with insight into what the potentials are for success.

WHO ARE THE TOP RATED BROKERS

ONLINE BROKERS

The following list relates to the parts of the world where English is the language of preference in business.

1) E*Trade Financial Network

2) TDWaterhouse.com

3) ShareBuilder.com

4) Fidelity.com

5) Ameritrade.com

6) Schwab.com

7) Datek.com

8) ML.com

9) CSFBDirect.com

10) Vanguard.com

11) Americanfunds.com

12) BuyandHold.com

13) EdwardJones.com

14) AmericanCentury.com

15) PutnamInvestments.com

16) Prudential.com

17) PruFN.com

18) TRowePrice.com

19) Janus.com

20) Scottrade.com

Although these rankings are believed to be accurate, it should be noted that there is a mix of different kinds of companies in the list. For example, it may not be fair to compare Vanguard with ShareBuilder.com. One is a mutual fund company and the other is a broker for non-mutual funds.

ONLINE BROKERAGE FIRMS

As online brokers do not concern themselves necessarily with the location of the customers, it is important to know who all of these online brokers are. In addition the following list includes their phone numbers for customer service purposes.

The following is a list of online brokerages and their phone numbers.

A.B. Watley
(888)229-2853
Action Direct (Royal Bank CA.)
(800)769-2583
Accutrade
(800)882-4887
Aftrader
(888)682-6973
American Century
(800)345-2021
American Express Financial Direct
(800)658-4677

Ameritrade.com
(800)454-9272
Andrew Peck Associates, Inc.
(800)221-5873
Atlantic Financial
(800)559-2900
ATradeUSA.com, Inc.)
(888)786-2545
Attain (All-Tech Direct, Inc.)
(877)528-8246
Attitude Online Trading

(888)889-9178

Banc of America Investment Services, Inc.

(800)765.4949

Bank One Corporation (Oneinvest.com)

(888)843-6382

Bank of Montreal (InvestorLine.com)

(800)387-7800

Belizebank Online (Off Shore)

(501) 2 72390

Benson York Group

(888)409-4773

Bidwell & Company

(800)547-6337

BlueStone Capital Partners, L.P.

(888)872-3367

BondAgent.com

(800)803-9052

Boom.com (Off Shore, Hong Kong)

(852)2255-8888

Brown & Company

(800)822-2021\

Bull & Bear Securities, Inc.

(800)262-5800

Cales Investments, Inc.

(303)765-5600

Castle Online

(888)276-5490

Charles Schwab & Co.

(800)372-4922

CitiBank.

(800)275-2424

Columbia Asset Management (USAFutures.com).

(800)435-9444

Comek Financial Group, Inc..

(800)844-9492

Commonwealth Bank of Australia (Off Shore).

61 2 8223 7014

Day-Trades.com.

(888)325-9300

Direct Trade Inc..

(800)756-0920

The Clark Financial Group

(800)243-2207

CompuTEL Securities

(800)432-0327

CyberCorp.com

(888)762-9237

Day Trading Net

(415)-331-2242

Datek

(888)-463-2835

Direct

(800)-327-1883

Direct Trade LLC

(888)-756-0920

DiscountBroker.com (Scottrade Securities)

(800)619-7283

1st Discount Brokerage
(888)-642-2811
Discover Brokerage Direct
(800)566-2273
DLJ Direct
(800)825-5723
Downstate Discount Brokerage, Inc.
(800)780-3543
Dreyfus Brokrage
(800)421-8395
EdgeTrade.com
(888)440-3343
Empire Financial Group, Inc.
(800)900-8101
Equity Trading Online, LLC
(877)388-7233
E-Trade
(888)387-2331
E-Trade Canada
(888)872-3388
The Executioner
(877)843-9999
Fidelity
(800)544-5555
Field Logan
(888)353-4353
The Financial Cafe
(877)600-6410
Financial Discounts Direct (Off Shore
UK) 01 420 549 090

Firefly Capital, Inc.
(888)883-3359
First American Discount Corporation
(Futures) (888)621-4415
First Financial Equity Corporation
(888)951-1010
First Midwest Securities, Inc.
(800)776-3004
Firstrade Securities Inc.
(888)988-6168
Fleet
(800)221-8210
FMS, Inc (Bonds, Tax Free
(800)367-2663
FOLIO[fn] Investments, Inc
(888)973-7890
Freedom Investments, Inc.
(800)381-1481
Freeman Welwood
(800)729-7585
Freetrade.com, Inc. (Ameritrade
Holding Corp.) (800)237-8692
Frontier Futures, Inc.
(800)278-6257
Garden State Securities Inc.
(877)477-7862
Global Access Financial Services
(888)366-8472
GlobalNeTrader
(800)467-5197
Globeshare Inc.

(877)456-2374

GRO Corporation

(800)852-3862

Harris InvestorLine

(800)621-0392

H&R Block Financial Corporation(Smart Vest)

(800)249-5500

HSBC Holdings plc (Off Shore)

(888)398-1180

IForex.net (Lincolnet Corp., Currencys)

(212)563-2100\

IJL Wachovia

(800)775-6547

Instant Futures, LLC

(877)583-9401

Interactive Brokers LLC

(203)618-5839

IntlTrader.com Inc.

(888)345-4685

Investex Securities Group, Inc.

(800)822-2050

InvesTrade

(800)498-7120

I-TRADEdirect.com

(888)783-3100

Jack White & Company

(800)233-3411

JB Oxford & Co.

(800)468-1876

JPR Capital

(800)577-2004

Key Bank, Brokerage

(800)553-2240

Killik & Co (Off Shore UK)

0870 606 1444

Levitt-Levitt

(800)671-8505

Lexit Capital LLC

(888)778-4998

Lieber & Weissman Securities, LLC

(800)261-9557

Lincolnet Corp.(Currencys)

(212)563-2100

Live Broker.com (Westminster Securities Corporation)

(800)553-6428

Livestreet.com

(516)873-4200

Man Direct (Off Shore UK)

0500 565 717

Mansion House Securities (F.E.) Ltd (Off Shore HK)

2843 1432

Marquette de Bary Co.

(800)221-3305

MAX Trade, L.L.C.

(888)741-8733

MB Trading

(866) 628-3001

McDonald Investments

(800)553-2240

Merrill Lynch, Pierce, Fenner & Smith Incorporated

(212)449-1000

Midwest Discount Brokers, Inc.

(800)397-0697

Morgan Stanley Dean Witter & Co.

(212)761-4000

Mr. Stock, Inc.>

(800)470-1896

MuniDirect.com, Inc.>

(888)432-6864

Muriel Siebert & Co.

(800)872-0711

My Discount Broker

(888)882-5600

National Discount Brokers

(800)888-3999

National Securities Corporation

(877)672-8723

Navillus Securities Inc.

(952)476-6002

Nestlerode & Co., Inc.

(814)238-6249

Net Bank

(800)553-9513

The Net Investor

(800)638-4250

Net-Invest.com, Inc.

(800)548-7796

Netstock Investment Corporation

(888)638-7865

Net Vest

(800)961-1500

Noble Trading

(877)872-3311

Now Trade

(877)669-8723

OLDE Discount Corporation

(800)872-6533

One Financial Center, Inc.

(877)554-6500

OnlineTrading.com

(800)995-1076

On-Site Trading Inc.

(888)402-0533

Patagon.com Securities Corp.

(888)539-8723

Pennaluna & Company

(800)535-5329

Penn Trade

(800)953-2860

Peremel & Company, Inc.

(800)737-3635

PowerStreet (Fidelity)

(800)544-5555

Preferred Capital Markets, Inc.

(888)889-9178

Preferred Technology

(888)781-0283

Prime Time Investment Services, Inc.

(800)545-6436

Princeton Daytrading, LLC
(888)665-9191
Professional Discount Securities
(800)478-6257
ProTrade Securities
(805)563-9017
Quick & Reilly
(800)453-2517
Real Fast Trader
(877) 286-9912
Regal Discount Securities
(800)786-9000
The R.J. Forbes Group
(800)754-7687
R.J. Thompson Securities Inc. (
RJT.com)
(800)927-0202
RML Trading
(888)765-4403
Royal Bank of Canada
(800)769-2583
Sanford Securities Limited (Off Shore
AU)
61 8 9321 1553
Savoy Discount Brokerage
(800)961-1500
Scotia Discount Brokerage Inc.
(Canadian) (800)263-3430

Scottrade
(800)619-7283

Self Trading Securities, Inc
(800)937-4162
Shochet Online
(888)227-9964
Sloan Securities Corp.
(201)592-9900
SmartVest (H&R Block Financial
Corporation)
(800)249-5500
Spear, Leeds & Kellogg
(800)395-6850
Speed Trader
(877)773-3357
STA Trading Services, Inc.
(800)781-0747
State Discount Brokers
(800)997-8283
StockPower Inc.
(877)430-7518
Stock Trade.net
(800)261-9557
Stockwalk.com, Inc.
(800)259-2800
Stocks 4 Less
(888)414-5377
Sovereign Securities
(888)882-5600
Summit Bank, Brokerage
(800)631-1635
Summit Trading, Inc.
(888)382-6552

Sunlogic Securities
(800)556-4600
SuperTrade USA, GlobaLink Securities,
(800)388-9788
SunTrust Internet Investing
(800)710-8208
Sure Trade (Quick and Reilly)
(800)837-7220
SwiftTrade;
(416) 351-0540
TD Waterhouse
(800)934-4448

Terra Nova Online
(866)866-6546
Thomas Cook (Business Only)
(800)522-2565
Thomas F. White and Company, Inc. (
White Discount Securities)
(800)669-4483
T. Rowe Price Discount Brokerage
(800)541-8803
Trade 4 Less
(800)780-3543
TradeCast Securities Ltd.
(877)303-7844
Trade.com
(888)872-3367
Trade Fast
(888)889-9178
Trade Portal

(888)839-2227
Traderight Corp.
(888)872-3335
Trade Scape
(800)467-7065
TradeStar Investments
(800)961-1500
Trading Direct
(212)766-0241
Trade-Well Discount Investing
(888)907-9797
Tru Trade
(800)328-8600
Unified Management Corporation
(888)862-7862
USAForce.com (USACapital, Inc.)
(888)483-6723
USAFutures.com (Columbia Asset
Management).
(800)435-9444
U.S. Bancorp Investments, Inc..
(800)872-2657
U.S. Invest
(213)653-1212
U.S. RICA Financial Inc.
(888)887-7422
Vanguard Brokerage Services
(800)662-7447
Vision Trade
(800)374-1940
Wachovia Securities, Inc.

(800)922-9008

Wall Street Access

(800)925-5781

The Wall Street Discount Corporation

(888)492-5578

Wall Street Electronica

(888)925-5783

Wall Street Equities Inc.

(800)321-4877

Wang Investments

(718)353-9264

Waterhouse Securities, Inc.

(800)934-4410

WealthHound Inc.

(877)947-8776

Web Street Securities

(800)932-8723

Wells Fargo

(800)872-3377

Westminster Securities Corporation

(800)553-6428

White Discount Securities

(800)669-4483

Wise Choice Discount

(800)490-6074

WIT Capital

(888)494-8227

WR Hambrecht + Co, LLC

(877)673-6476

Wyse Securities

(800)640-8668

Yamner & Company, Inc.

(800)221-5676

York Securities, Inc.

(800)221-3154

XpressTrade, LLC

(800)947-6228

Ziegler Thrift Trading Inc.

(612)333-4206

PRIME (FULL SERVICE) BROKERS

These are the top rated full service brokers in the parts of the world where English is the language of preference. Most of these companies have offices in the markets where the major exchanges are located. For example these companies serve exchanges in Asia, Europe, and the Middle East.

1) JP Morgan Chase

2) Bank of America

3) Barclays Capital

4) Bear Stearns

5) Citigroup

6) Credit Suisse First Boston

7) Deutsche Bank

8) Dresdner Klienwort Wasserstein

9) Fidelity Investments

10) Goldman Sachs

11) Jefferies Securities

12) Lehman Brothers

13) Merlin Securities

14) Merrill Lynch

15) Morgan Stanley

16) Pershing LLC

17) UBS

FULL SERVICE BROKERAGES LIST

This is a list of the full service brokerages in major geographical markets in the USA. Brokerages originating in other countries are also listed as the USA office.

AB Wong Capital, LLC New York
212-480-2127
AMRO, Inc. Chicago 312-904-2000
AFA Financial Group, Calabasas, CA
626-744-2580
Affinity Investment, Basking Ridge, NJ
908-860-3930
AFG Securities, Toronto Ontario
416-367-1900

AIG Equity Sales, New York
212-770-5371
Allegiance Capital, South Portland, ME
207-879-2352
Allen & Company, New York
212-832-8000

Alliance Capital Management, New York
212-969-1000
Alison-Williams, Minneapolis, MN
612-3333-3475
Allstate Financial, Lincoln, NE
402-328-5752
Amaranth Global, Greenwich CT
203-422-3300
America's Growth Capital, Boston
617-261-4100
American Century Brokerage Mountain
View, CA 816-521-5575
American Realty Capital Markets,
Richmond 804-897-9399
Ameriprise Financial Services,
Minneapolis 612-671-3131

Ameritas Investment Lincoln, NE
402-467-6920

Anderson & Strudwick, Richmond
804-643-2400

Andrew Garrett, New York
212-682-8833

Arthurs, Lestrange, Pittsburgh
412-306-1730

Asian Pacific, Hagatna, Guam
671-472-6400

Associated Securities, Los Angeles
310-670-0800

Auerbach Grayson, New York
212-557-4444

Backstrom McCarley Berry, San
Francisco 415-433-0270

Robert W. Baird, Milwaukee
414-0765-35000

Baker & Co, Rocky River, OH
216-696-0167

Banc of America, New York
888-583-8900

Banca Securities, New York
212-326-1100

Banco Do Brasil, New York
212-626-7206

Banif Securities, New York
212-487-1800

Barclays Capital, New York
212-412-4000

Barnard Jacobs Mellet, Stamford, CT
203-973-2888

Barron Moore, Dallas 214-520-6500

M.R. Beal, New York 212-983-3930

Bear Stearns, New York 212-272-2000

Berkshire Capital, New York
212-207-1000

Blackmont Captial, Tornoto, Ontario
416-864-3600

William Blair, Chicago 312-236-16000

Bloomberg Tradebook, New York
212-617-5555

BMO Nesbitt Burns, Toronto, Ontario
416-359-4000

BNY Brokerage, New York
212-841-3000

BOE Securities, Philadelphia
215-458-5500

W.J. Bonfanti, New York 212-808-0004

Brean Murray Carret, New York
212-593-3800

Brimberg, New York 212-333-5400

Brinson Patrick, New York
212-453-5000

Brown Advisory, Baltimore
410-537-5400

Brown Brothers Harriman, New York
212-483-1818

Bulltick, Mexico D.F. 305-533-1541

Burnham, New Yorkm 212-262-3100

Cabrera Capital, Chicago 312-236-8888

Caylon Securities, New York
212-408-5700
Cambridge, New York 212-826-3030
Cameron Murphy & Spangler,
Pasadena 626-449-1323
Canaccord Capital, Vancouver
604-643-7300
Cantor Fitzgerald, New York
212-938-5000
The Capital Group, New York
12-581-5000
Carey Financial, New York
212-492-1100
Carlin Equities, New York 212-218-8839
Cary Street Partners, Richmond
804-340-8100
Cascade Financial, Denver
303-292-1121
Casey Professional, San Francisco
415-544-9100
Casimir Capital, New York
212-798-1300
Quincy Cass, Los Angelesw
310-473-4411
Caymus Partners, Atlanta 404-995-8300
Casenove Inc., New York 212-376-1225
Centennial Securities, Grand Rapids
616-942-7680
Chapdelaine Corpoate, New York
212-208-9120
Charles River, Burlington, MA

781-425-6403
Chase Investment, Chicago
312-732-6058
Chelsea Financial, Staten Island
718-967-8400
Chittenden Securities, Burlington, VT
800-851-0476
Churchill Financial, Louisville, KY
501-893-1780
CIBC World Markets, New York
212-856-4000
Citadel Investments, Chicago
312-395-2100
Citicorp Investment Services, Long
Island City, NY 212-559-1000
Citigroup Global Markets, New York
212-816-6000
Clifden Equities, New York
212-259-2610
Comercia Securities, Detroit
313-222-0012
Contemporary Financial Solutions, West
Palm Beach 800-709-9982

Corinthian Partners, New York
212-287-1552
Cowen and Company, New York
646-562-1000
Credit Suisse, New York 212-325-2000
Crowell Weedon, Los Angeles 213-620-
1850

Cuscathlan Securities, Guatemala
022-502-2250-2040

Cypress Associates, New York
212-682-2222

Daiwa Securities, New York
212-612-700

DAV/Wetherly Financial, Los Angeles
310-773-0074

Davenport and Company, Richmond
804-780-2000

David Adams Capital Markets, New
York 646-432-6300

Davy Securities Limited, Dublin
3531-61458778

JV Delaney Associates, Newport Beach
949-720-0063

Deutsche Bank Securities, New York
212-250-2500

Dominick & Dominick, New York
212-558-8800

Doresey & Company, New Orleans
504-524-5431

Dresdner Kleinwort Wasserstein, New
York 212-969-2700

Dreihaus Securities, Chicago
312-587-3800

Duff & Phelps Securities, Chicago
312-697-4600

du Pasquier & Co, New York
212-898-7500

Edgemont Capital, New York

212-867-8935

AG Edwards, St. Louis 314-955-3000

EHY Securities, New York
212-479-2647

Electronic Global Securities, New York
212-286-1245

Equibase Capital Markets, Chicago
773-489-7600

ESN North America, New York
212-715-4524

Allen C. Ewing, Jacksonville, FL
904-354-5573

Exane, New York 212-634-4990

FBTY Investments, New Orleans
504-584-5888

Federated Securities, Pittsburgh
412-2888-1900

Feldstein Financial Group, Chester, NJ
908-879-9559

Ferris Baker Watts, Washington, DC
202-661-9500

Fidelity Brokerage, Boston
617-563-7000

Fifth Third Securities, Cincinnati
513-358-5925

Firmat USA, New York 646-557-9000

Financial Counseling, Dallas
214-750-4400

Financorp Group International, New
York 212-407-0300

Fintech Securities, Atlanta

770-396-2256

First Allied Securitier, San Diego
619-702-9600

First Bermuda Securities, Hamilton
Bermuda 441-295-1330

1st Global Capital, Dallas 214-265-1201

First Investors Corporation, New York
212-858-8000

First Matrix, Denver 303-932-4278

First Republic Securities, San Francisco
415-296-5885

First Southwest, Dallas 214-953-4000

First Washington, Seattle 206-624-8320

FNY Management, New York
212-848-0600

Folger Nolan Fleming Douglas,
Washington, DC 202-783-5252

Foresters Equity, San Diego
858-550-4844

Fox-Pitt Kelton, New York 212-687-1106

Fremont Capital, San Francisco
415-284-8932

GC Securities, Atlanta 404-816-7540

Gagnon Securities, New York
212-554-5050

The Garbacz Group, St. Louis
314-991-1303

Gardner Rich, Chicago 312-992-3333

GE Capital Markets, Stanford, CT
203-357-4194

Gelber Securities, Chicago

312-427-7100

Gerogeson Shareholders Securities,
New York 212-440-9920

Gerson Lehman Group, New York
212-838-3660

Girard Securities, San Diego
858-622-2140

Giulani Capital Advisors, Chicago
312-756-3800

Globalvest Group, Laguna Niquel, CA
949-466-6461

JA Glynn, St. Louis 314-997-1277

Goldman Sachs, New York
212-902-1000

Greenberg Financial, Tucson
520-544-4909

Gunnallen Financial, Tampa
800-713-4046

H & R Block, Detroit 313-628-1200

WR Hambrecht, San Francisco
-551-8600

John Hancock Funds, Boston
617-663-3000

Hapoalim Securiteis, New York
212-898-6200

Harris Associates, Chicago
312-621-0600

Harris Nesbitt, New York 212-702-1200

Hattier Sanford & Reynoir, Memphis
800-582-2296

Haywood Securities, Vancouver

604-697-7170
HBK Global, New York 212-588-5100
Heflin & Company, Los Angeles
310-229-9700
Hefren-Tilotson, Pittsburgh
412-434-0990

Heidtke & Company, Nashville
615-254-0992
Hibernia Investments, New Orleans
504-533-5259
Horowitz & Associates, Northbrook, IL
847-790-1400
Howe Barnes, Chicago 312-655-3000
HSBC Securities, New York
212-525-6120
Wayne Hummer, Chicago 312-431-1700
Hunter Associates, Pittsburgh
412-471-4191
HVB Capital, New York 212-672-6000
Hybrid Trading, Wheat Ridge, CO
303-600-2501
IDB Captial, New York 212-551-8800
IFL Capital, New York 212-209-2115
Incapital, Chicago 312-379-3700
ING Advisors Network, Atlanta
404-841-6800
ING Financial Markets, New York
212-309-8200
Instinet Group, New York 212-310-9500

Integrated Trading and Investments, Las
Vegas 702-360-0011
InvesstPrivate, New York 212-739-7700
Itau Securities, New York 212-207-9056
Janney Montgomery Scott, Philadelphia
215-665-6000
Jefferies Group, New York
212-284-2300
Johnston Lemon, Washington, DC
202-842-5500
Kahn Brothers, New York 212-980-5050
Keefe Bruvette & Woods, New York
800-966-1559
Knight Equity Markets, Jersey City
800-544-7508
JW Korth, Miami 305-668-8485
Kovack Securities, Fort Lauderdale
866-564-6574
Kovitz Securities, Chicago
312-334-7300
LeBranche & Co, New York
212-425-1144

Ladenburg Thalmann, New York
212-409-2000
Lambright Financial, Chicago
212-739-0038
Emmett Larkin, San Francisco
415-985-2332
Lava Trading, New York 212-609-0113
Lazard Capital Markets, New York

212-632-6050

Lazard Freres & Co, New York
212-632-6000

Legacy Securities, Atlanta
404-985-2420

Legg Mason, Baltimore 410-539-0000

Lehman Brothers, New York
212-526-7000

Leprerca de Neuflize/Tocqueville, New
York 212-698-0800

Leumi Investment, New York
212-407-4353

Lightstone, New York 866-793-8700

Linsco/Private Ledger, Boston 800-
775-4575

Loeb Partners, New York 212=483-7000

Loewen Ondaatie McCutcheon,
Toronto, Ontario 416-964-4455

Lombard, Baltimore 410-342-1300

M&A Capital Advisers, Las Vegas
702-851-3585

Macquarie Securities, New York
212-231-1000

Madison Avenue, San Diego
868-357-2920

Bernard Madoff, New York
212-230-2424

Maine Securities, Portland, ME
207-775-0800

Majestic Securities, New York
646-442-6306

Man Securities, Chicago 312-663-7500

Manarin Securities, Omaha
402-330-1168

Maplewood Investment, Dallas
214-739-5677

Matrix Capital Group, New York
212-652-3290

McFadden Farrell Smith, New York
212-618-0905

McNally Financial, San Antonio
210-545-7080

MDB Capital Group, Santa Monica
310-562-5000

Mellon Securities, Chicago
312-456-7300

Melvin Securities, Chicago
312-341-0050

Merrill Lynch, New York 212-449-1000

Midwood Securities, New York
212-742-9600

Miller Tabel & Company, New York
212-370-0040

Moors & Cabot, Boston 617-426-0500

JP Morgan Securities, New York
212-270-6000

Morgan Stanley, New York
212-761-4000

Mufson Howe Hunter, Philadelphia
215-399-5413

Murphy & Durieu, New York
212-618-0900

Nafinsa Securities, New York
646-485-5172
NatCity Investments, Cleveland
216-222-9590
Natexis Bleichroeder, New York
212-698-3000
National Australia Capital, New York
877-377-5480
National Bank Financial, Montreal
514-879-2222
National Securities, Seattle
800-552-7574
Needham & Company, New York
323-371-8300
Martin Nelson, Seattle 206-682-6261
Nevis Securities, Atlanta 678-298-2006
NevWest Securities, Las Vegas
702-257-4660
New England Securities, Boston
800-225-7670
New York Global, New York
212-791-2920
Nollenberger Capital, San Francisco
415-402-6000
Normura Securities, New York
212-667-9300
Northern Trust, Chicago 312-557-3096
Northwestern Mutual Investment,
Milwaukee 866-664-7737
David A Noyes, Chicago 312-782-0400
Nuveen Investments, Chicago

312-917-7700
William O'Neil & Company, Los Angeles
310-448-6800
Oppenheimer & Company, New York
212-668-8000
Overture Securities, New York
212-624-1900
Pacific American, San Deigo
858-320-2850
Pacific International, Vancouver
604-664-2900
Park Avenue Securities, New York
888-482-7342
Penson Financial Services, Dallas
214-765-1100
Peters & Company, Calgary, Alberta
403-261-4850
Petersen Investments, New York
212-363-4300
Piper Jaffray, Minneapolis
612-303-6000
PNC Investments, Pittsburgh
412-762-6469
Podesta & Company, Chicago
312-899-0133
Portfolio Resources, 305-372-0299
Prospect Finanical, Los Angeles
310-231-5648
Propsera Financial, Dallas
872-581-3000
Prudential Equity Group, New York

212-778-6806
Putnam, Boston 617-292-1000
Putnam Lovell, New York 212-546-7500
Quadriserve Securities, New York
212-905-5225

Raymond James, St. Petersberg
727-567-1000
WH Reaves, Jersey City 201-332-4596
Redwood Brokerage, New York
212-361-1630
Register & Akers, Atlanta 404-364-2180
Reserv Partners, New York
212-401-5500
Rhodes Securities, Fort Worth
817-334-0455
Richards, Merrill & Peterson, Spokane
509-624-3214
Robeco USA, New York 212-908-9500
Frank Russell, Tacoma 888-751-8354
S&Y Asset, San Francisco
415-435-2900
SAFDII Investment, New York
212-457-8600
Sagent Advisors, New York
212-904-9400
Samco Financial, Phoenix
602-230-9372
Sanders Morris Harris, Houston
713-224-3100
Sarli Financial, New York 212-216-9727

Satuma Brokerage, Bellingham, WA
360-734-1266
Schottenfeld Group, New York
212-300-2200
Charles Schwab, San Francisco
415-627-7000
Scotia Capital USA, New York
212-225-6500
Scott-Macon, New York 212-755-8200
Scott & Stingfellow, Richmond
804-643-1811
Securian Financial, St. Paul
888-237-1838
Senvest International, New York
212-977-2466
SG Amereicas Securities, New York
212-278-6189
Signature Securities, New York
866-744-5463
Simmon First, Little Rock 501-223-4321

EH Smith Jacobs, New York
212-742-8130
WM Smith, Denver 303-831-9696
Soleil Securities, New York
212-380-4800
Sorrento Pacific, San Deigo
858-805-7916
Soverign Securities, Philadelphia
267-256-2818
SPARX Securities, New York

212-452-5000

Spencer Clarke, New York

212-446-6100

Stanford Group, Houston 713-964-8300

State Street Global, Boston

617-786-3000

Stifel Nicolaus, St. Louis 314-342-2000

Stillpoint Wealth Management, Atlanta

404-467-0585

Stonnington Group, Los Angeles

213-683-4511

Strasbeourger Pearson Tulcin Wolff,

New York 212-952-7500

Strategic Financial, Atlanta

678-274-1850

Strategic Point, Providence

401-273-1500

SunTrust Capital, Atlanta 404-724-3389

Swiss American, New York

212-612-8700

SWS Group, Dallas 214-859-1800

Syndicated Capital, Santa Monica

310-255-4490

T Rowe Price, Baltimore 410-345-2000

TD Ameritrade, Omaha 800-237-8692

TD Securities, New York 212-827-7300

Terwin Capital, New York 212-218-5800

ThinkEquity, San Francisco

415-249-2900

Thomas Group, Atlanta 678-539-1700

Thrivent Investment, Minneapolis

612-340-8648

Toussaint Capital, New York

212-514-5176

Tradelink, Chicago 312-264-2198

Tradition Asiel Securities, New York

212-791-4500

Tribeca Securities, New York

212-219-9096

TS Phillips, Oklahoma City

05-943-9433

Twenty First Securities, New York

212-418-6000

UBS Financial Weehawken

201-352-3000

CE Unterberg Towbin, New York

212-389-8000

UNX, Burbank 818-333-3000

USAllianz Securities, Minneapolis

888-446-5872

Vanguard Capital, LaJolla 858-455-5070

VECTORMEX, New York 212-407-5500

HD Vest, Irving, TX 972-870-6000

Viscogliosi, New York 212-583-9700

Vista Research Brokerage, New York

212-439-4200

Wachovia Capital, Charlotte

704-383-5018

Wachovia Securities, Richmond

800-627-8625

Walnut Street, St. Louis 877-925-6881

Wedbush Morgan, Los Angeles

213-688-8000

Christopher Weil, San Deigo

858-704-1444

Tomas Weisel, San Francisco

415-364-2500

Wells Fargo Securities, San Francisco

415-954-8351

West LB Securities, New York

212-403-3900

Westrock Advisors, New York

212-922-1995

JN Whipple, Chicago 312-782-3725

Whitehorne and Company, Newport, CA

949-796-9346

White Mountain, New York

212-509-0313

Williams Capital, New York

212-830-4500

Williams Financial, Dallas 972-661-8700

Winchester Group, New York

212-486-8181

Woodmen Financial, Omaha

402-997-7985

Worthmark Financial, St. Paul

877-814-2385

XE Capital Securities, New York

646-253-6400

Yeild Quest, Atlanta 404-446-3370

Ziegler Companies, Milwaukee

414-978-6400

Zions First National Bank, Salt Lake City

801-524-4640

Ziz Investment, Chicago 312-427-7208

OTHER IMPORTANT MARKET INFORMATION

PROGRAM TRADING

Program trading is defined as the use of computers in stock markets to engage in protection of portfolio through automatic trade orders. More precisely, the New York Stock Exchange defines a program trade as a basket of stocks having either a total value of $1M (or more) and where the total number of stocks in the basket is 15 or greater.

Program trades need to be specifically marked as such when submitted to the exchanges, and there are certain restrictions placed on programs that do not apply to non-program trades. These were put in place after the market fall in October of 1987.

The most popular explanation for the 1987 crash was selling by program traders. Many blamed program trading strategies for blindly selling stocks as markets fell, exacerbating the decline.

MARKET MAKER

A market maker is a person or a firm which quotes a buy and sell price in a financial instrument or commodity hoping to make a profit on the *turn* or the *bid/offer spread*.

Most stock exchanges operate on a *matched bargain* or *order driven* basis. In such a system there are no designated or official market makers but market makers nevertheless exist. When a buyer's bid meets a seller's offer (or vice versa) the stock exchange's matching system will decide that a deal has been executed.

In the United States, the New York Stock Exchange (NYSE) and American Stock Exchange (AMEX), among others, have a single exchange member, known as the "specialist," that acts as the official market maker for a given security. In return for providing a required amount of liquidity to the security's market, being on the other side of trades when there are short-term buy-and-sell-side imbalances in customer orders, and attempting to prevent excess volatility, the specialist is granted various informational and trade execution advantages.

Other U.S. exchanges, most prominently the NASDAQ Stock Exchange, employ several competing official market makers in a security. These market makers are required to maintain two-sided markets during exchange hours and are obligated to buy and sell at their displayed bids and offers. They typically do not receive the trading advantages a specialist does, but they do get some, such as the ability to "naked short" a stock, i.e. selling it without a borrow. In most situations only official market makers are permitted to engage in naked shorting.

On the London Stock Exchange (LSE) there are official market makers for many securities (but not for shares in the largest and most heavily traded companies, which instead use an automated system SETS.) Some of the LSE's member firms take on the obligation of always making a two way price in each of the stocks in which they make markets. It is their prices which are displayed on the Stock Exchange Automated Quotation system, and it is with them that ordinary stockbrokers generally have to deal when buying or selling stock on behalf of their clients.

Proponents of the official market making system claim market makers add to the liquidity and depth of the market by taking a short or long position for a time, thus assuming some risk, in return for hopefully making a small profit. On the LSE one can always buy and sell stock: each stock always has at least two market makers and they are obliged to deal.

This contrasts with some of the smaller order driven markets. On the Johannesburg Stock Exchange, for example, it can be very difficult to determine at what price one would be able to buy or sell even a small block of any of the many illiquid stocks because there are often no buyers or sellers on the order board. However, there is no doubting the liquidity of the big order driven markets in the U.S.

Unofficial market makers are free to operate on order driven markets or, indeed, on the LSE. They do not have the obligation to always be making a two way price but they do not have the advantage that everyone must deal with them either.

IMPORTANT FINANCIAL THEORIES AND HYPOTHESIS

Some may not think this subject important to a discussion regarding a stock broker. In fact, while sophtisticated financial theories can bore one to sleep very quickly, a cursory understanding of at least the definition of the theories and hypothosis is important for a general and complete understanding.

The efficient market hypothesis (EMH) asserts that financial markets are "efficient", or that prices on traded assets, e.g. stocks, bonds, or property, already reflect all known information and therefore are accurate in the sense that they reflect the collective beliefs of all investors about future prospects.

The efficient market hypothesis implies that it is not possible to consistently outperform the market - appropriately adjusted for risk - by using any information that the market already knows, except through luck or obtaining and trading on inside information. It further suggests that the future flow of news (that which will determine future stock prices) is random and unknowable in the present.

EMH allows that when faced with new information, some investors may overreact and some may underreact. All that is required by the EMH is that investors' reactions be random enough that the net effect on market prices cannot be reliably exploited to make an abnormal profit. Under EMH, the market may, in fact, behave irrationally for a long period of time. Crashes, bubbles and depressions are all consistent with efficient market hypothesis, so long as this irrational behavior is not predictable or exploitable.

There are three common forms in which the efficient market hypothesis is commonly stated - weak form efficiency, semi-strong form efficiency and strong form efficiency, each of which have different implications for how markets work.

WEAK-FORM EFFICIENCY

No excess returns can be earned by using investment strategies based on historical share prices or other financial data.

Weak-form efficiency implies that no Technical analysis techniques will be able to consistently produce excess returns.

In a weak-form efficient market current share prices are the best, unbiased, estimate of the value of the security. Theoretical in nature, weak form efficiency advocates assert that fundamental analysis can be used to identify stocks that are undervalued and overvalued. Therefore, keen investors looking for profitable companies can earn profits by researching financial statements.

SEMI-STRONG FORM EFFICIENCY

Share prices adjust instantaneously and in an unbiased fashion to publicly available new information, so that no excess returns can be earned by trading on that information. Semi-strong-form efficiency implies that Fundamental analysis techniques will not be able to reliably produce excess returns.

To test for semi-strong-form efficiency, the adjustments to previously unknown news must be of a reasonable size and must be instantaneous. To test for this, consistent upward or downward adjustments after the initial change must be looked for. If there are any such adjustments it would suggest that investors had interpreted the information in a biased fashion and hence in an inefficient manner.

STRONG-FORM EFFICIENCY

Share prices reflect all information and no one can earn excess returns.

To test for strong form efficiency, a market needs to exist where investors cannot consistently earn excess returns over a long period of time. When the topic of insider trading is introduced, where an investor trades on information that is not yet publicly available, the idea of a strong-form efficient market seems impossible. Studies on the US stock market have shown that people do trade on inside information. It was also found though that others monitored the activity of those with inside information and in turn followed, having the effect of reducing any profits that could be made.

Even though many fund managers have consistently beaten the market, this does not necessarily invalidate strong-form efficiency. We need to find out how many managers in fact do beat the market, how many match it, and how many underperform it. The results imply that performance relative to the market is more or less normally distributed, so that a certain percentage of managers can be expected to beat the market. Given that there are tens of thousand of fund managers worldwide, then having a few dozen star performers is perfectly consistent with statistical expectations.

ARGUMENTS CONCERNING THE VALIDITY OF THE EMH HYPOTHESIS

Some observers dispute the notion that markets behave consistently with the efficient market hypothesis, especially in its stronger forms. Some economists, mathematicians and market practitioners cannot believe that man-made markets are strong-form efficient when there are prima facie reasons for inefficiency including the slow diffusion of information, the relatively great power of some market participants (e.g. financial institutions), and the existence of apparently sophisticated professional investors.

The efficient market hypothesis was introduced in the late 1960s. Prior to that, the prevailing view was that markets were inefficient. Inefficiency was commonly believed to exist e.g. in the United States and United Kingdom stock markets.

It may be that professional and other market participants who have discovered reliable trading rules or stratagems see no reason to divulge them to academic researchers. It might be that there is an information gap between the academics who study the markets and the professionals who work in them. Some observers point to seemingly inefficient features of the markets that can be exploited e.g seasonal tendencies and divergent returns to assets with various characteristics. Factor analysis and studies of returns to different types of investment strategies suggest that some types of stocks may outperform the market long-term (e.g in the UK, the USA and Japan).

To a market participant, the difficulty of proving the hypothesis unequivocally also leads to the question of whether or not economists should bother with the term "hypothesis", and should perhaps move to a more accurate "point of discussion". "Hypothesis" could then be left to the natural sciences, where it serves an active function, rather than serving to elevate a broad and unsubstantiable guess.

Regardless of the validity of the EMH, there exists a small number of investors who have outperformed the market over long periods of time, including Peter Lynch, Warren Buffett, and Bill Miller.

ALTHERNATIVE THEORY OF BEHAVIORAL FINANCE

Opponents of the EMH sometimes cite examples of market movements that seem inexplicable in terms of conventional theories of stock price determination, for example the stock market crash of October 1987 where most stock exchanges crashed at the same time. It is virtually impossible to explain the scale of those market falls by reference to any news event at the time. The explanation may lie either in the mechanics of the exchanges (e.g. no safety nets to discontinue trading initiated by program sellers) or the peculiarities of human nature.

Behavioural psychology approaches to stock market trading are among some of the more promising alternatives to EMH (and some investment strategies seek to exploit exactly such inefficiencies). A growing field of research called behavioral finance studies how cognitive or emotional biases, which are individual or collective, create anomalies in market prices and returns that may be inexplicable via EMH alone.

CORPORATE GOVERNANCE

While it may seem that this topic doesn't belong in an ebook about stockbrokers, the reality is that it is a very important subject to every stockbroker. The reason is is that corporate governance is what "governs" what a public company (corporation) does and how they report their financials.

Parties involved in corporate governance include the governing or regulatory body (e.g. the U.S. Securities and Exchange Commission), the Chief Executive Officer, the board of directors, management and shareholders. Other stakeholders who take part include suppliers, employees, creditors, customers and the community at large.

In corporations, the principal (shareholder) delegates decision rights to the agent (manager) to act in the principal's best interests. This separation of ownership from control implies a loss of effective control by shareholders over managerial decisions. Partly as a result of this separation between the main two parties, a system of corporate governance controls is implemented to assist in aligning the incentives of managers with those of shareholders, in order to limit the self-satisfying opportunities for managers.

A board of directors often plays a key role in corporate governance. It is their responsibility to endorse the organization's strategy, develop directional policy, appoint, supervise and remunerate senior executives and to ensure accountability of the organization to its owners and authorities. \

All parties to corporate governance have an interest, whether direct or indirect, in the effective performance of the organization. Directors, workers and management receive salaries, benefits and reputation; whilst shareholders receive capital return. Customers receive goods and services; suppliers receive compensation for their goods or services. In return these individuals provide value in the form of natural, human, social and other forms of capital.

The term corporate governance has come to mean many things. It may describe:

The processes by which companies are directed and controlled

Encouragement of companies' compliance with codes (as in corporate governance guidelines)

Investment technique based on active ownership (as in corporate governance funds)

A field in economics, which studies the many issues arising from the separation of ownership and control

At its broadest, corporate governance encompasses the framework of rules, relationships, systems and processes within and by which fiduciary authority is exercised and controlled in corporations. Relevant rules include applicable laws of the land as well as internal rules of a corporation. Relationships include those between all related parties, the most important of which are the owners, managers, directors of the board (when such entity exists), regulatory authorities and to a lesser extent employees and the community at large. Systems and processes deal with matters such as delegation of authority, performance measures, assurance mechanisms, reporting requirements and accountabilities.

In this way, the corporate governance structure spells out the rules and procedures for making decisions on corporate affairs. It also provides the structure through which the company objectives are set, as well as the means of attaining and monitoring the performance of those objectives.

Issues of fiduciary duty and accountability are often discussed within the framework of corporate governance.

As a result of the separation of stakeholder influence from control in modern organizations, a system of corporate governance controls is implemented on behalf of stakeholders to reduce agency costs and information asymmetry. Corporate governance is used to monitor whether outcomes are in accordance with plans; and to motivate the organization to be more fully informed in order to maintain or alter organizational activity. Primarily though, corporate governance is the mechanism by which individuals are motivated to align their actual behaviours with the overall corporate good (ie maximum aggregate value generated by the organization and shared fairly amongst all participants).

Credits and Acknowledgements

Special thanks are given to Kent Capener for his assistance in reviewing the draft documents and for his kind comments. I am deeply grateful to my wife, Shajida for the encouragement and ongoing support. She has helped to bring focus and meaningfulness in many areas of my life.

Finally, I am eternally indebted to my late mother, Roshomala Khatun for loving and caring for me. Her presence has brought proper guidance in my life without which I would be wondering like a helpless child.

Glossary Of Financial Terms

The following glossary is not a complete glossary of the investment marketplace. However, it should be sufficient for any one's needs on a regular basis.

Accredited investor

Someone who is supposed to know a lot about investing, and who meets certain income and net worth criteria, as established by the SEC ($1,000,000). Being an "accredited investor" is sometimes a requirement for certain limited partnership investments and in "private placements".

Accrual basis

An accounting method where income is reported when earned and expenses are reported when incurred. This is in contrast to cash-basis accounting, which reports income when it is actually received and expenses when they're actually paid.

Accumulation

Buying shares over a period of time. For an individual investor, this just means buying additional shares of a stock you already own. For an institution, however, it may mean making a series of purchases rather than one large purchase that could drive up the market price.

Accumulation period

In retirement parlance, the years when one is making regular contributions to a retirement plan or deferred annuity. The period is considered to end when the income payments begin.

Acquisition of assets

A merger or consolidation deal when an acquirer buys a company's assets.

Active management

Any investment strategy that involves picking individual securities with the goal of either beating the market's returns, or lessening the risk of following the market. In the context of mutual funds, active management refers to any non-index funds.

Aggressive growth fund

A mutual fund that seeks long-term capital growth by investing primarily in stocks of fast growing smaller companies or narrow market segments, such as "the technology sector" or "the Internet sector." Sometimes called a capital appreciation fund.

American Depositary Receipt (ADR)

A receipt for the shares of a foreign-based company held by a U.S. bank that entitles the shareholder to all dividends and capital gains of the underlying stock. ADRs trade similar to stocks on U.S. exchanges, and provide a way for Americans to invest in foreign-based companies by buying their shares in the U.S. instead of through an overseas exchange.

American Stock Exchange (or Amex or AMEX)

Founded in 1842 in New York City, the American Stock Exchange is one of the three major stock exchanges in the U.S.

Amount recognized

The amount of a capital gain that is reportable and subject to tax.

Analyst

A financial professional who analyzes securities to determine their investment merits, including possibly a "fair" or "intrinsic" value for them. The term is generally applied to almost any professional investor who does research of some kind. There are "sell-side" and "buy-side" analysts. "Sell-side" analysts typically work for investment banks and brokerages and sell or publish their analysis. "Buy-side" analysts typically work for the mutual fund companies or institutions that use the analysis to make investment decisions for the funds they manage.

Annual effective yield

The measure of the actual annual rate of return on an account after interest is compounded.

Annual report

This is the corporate financial statement that shareholders eagerly wait for each year. These reports are required by Securities and Exchange Commission regulations.

Annualize

To make a period of less than a year apply to a full year to facilitate comparative analysis. For example, to annualize quarterly results, you multiply them by four. \

Annuity

This is a contract between an insurance company and a person that provides for periodic payments to the individual or designated beneficiary in return for an investment. Typically, an annuity agrees to provide payments to the purchaser of the contract (annuitant) beginning at some point in the future.

Appreciation

This is an increase in the price or value of an asset. Appreciation is one component of total return.

Ask

This is the price at which a prospective seller is willing to sell a security.

Asset

An asset is anything that has monetary value. Typical personal assets include stocks, real estate, jewelry, art, cars, and bank accounts. Corporate assets are found on the company's balance sheet and include cash, accounts receivable, short- and long-term investments, inventories, and prepaid expenses.

Asset allocation

Dividing investment dollars among various asset classes, typically among cash investments, bonds, and stocks. Wall Street firms frequently change their "model asset allocation" portfolios -- ostensibly to show that they have recalculated the best method for balancing the risks involved in holding various investments.

Asset allocation fund

A mutual fund that, as market conditions change, consistently rebalances its investments among the major asset classes (stocks, cash, and bonds).

Asset classes

The three major asset classes are cash (also called cash reserves, money market instruments), bonds, and stocks.

Automatic reinvestment

A method in which the dividends or other earnings from an investment are used to buy additional shares in the investment vehicle. Dividend Reinvestment Plans (Drips) are one example.

Average maturity

The average of all maturity dates for securities in a money market or bond fund. The longer the average maturity, the more volatile a fund's share price will be, moving up or down as interest rates change -- which they do every day.

Back-end load

A pernicious and usually not fully explained sales fee charged by some mutual funds when an investor sells fund shares. Also called a contingent deferred sales charge.

Balanced fund

This is where a mutual fund provides a combination of stocks, bonds, and/or money market instruments.

Basis point

Most often used relating to changes in interest rates. One basis point is 1/100 of a percentage point.

Bear

When a person is generally pessimistic about market outlook or has a pessimistic view on a sector or specific stock, they are a bear or bearish.

Bear market

When the overall market loses value over an extended period of time. There is no "official" definition of what makes a bear market, though many feel a drop of at least 10% is needed. A drop of something less than 10% is often called a "correction".

Beta

This is a measure of the relative volatility of a stock or other security as compared to the volatility of the entire market (usually measured by the S&P 500 index). A beta above 1.0 shows greater volatility than the overall market, and a beta below 1.0 is less volatile.

Bid

The price a prospective buyer is willing to pay for a security.

Bid-ask spread (or "the spread")

The difference between what a buyer is willing to pay (bid) for a security and the seller's asking price (ask).

Blue-chip stocks

These are "the" large companies -- often Dow components -- that have been around long enough to have a solid history of rewarding shareholders. Think Coca-Cola, IBM, General Electric, General Motors, and Johnson & Johnson, etc.

Board of directors

A group of people elected by a corporation's shareholders to oversee the management of the company. The board members meet several times each year, are paid in cash and/or stock, and take on legal responsibility for corporate activities.

Bond

This is an interest bearing or discounted debt security issued by corporations and governments. Bonds are essentially loans by the investor to the issuer in return for interest payments.

Bond fund

This is a mutual fund that invests in bonds.

Book value

This is a company's total assets minus any liabilities and intangible assets. Book value is literally the value of a company that can be found in the accounting ledger and is often represented as a per-share value by taking the company's shareholder equity and dividing by the current number of shares outstanding.

Bottom line

The bottom line on a business's income statement shows its actual profits according to generally accepted accounting principles (GAAP).

Broker

One who sells financial products. Whether in insurance, real estate, or stocks, most full service brokers work under commission structures that can be at direct odds with the best interests of their clients.

Bull

This is a person with a positive or optimistic outlook for the general market, a market segment or industry, or for particular stocks (e.g., a Coca-Cola bull).

Bull market

This is a market that has been gaining value over a prolonged period.

Buy-and-hold

A strategy that employs buying shares of companies with the intention of keeping them for a long time, preferably indefinitely, and participating in the long-term success of being a partial owner of the business underlying the stock.

Call option

An option contract that grants the buyer the right, but not the obligation, to buy the optioned shares of a company at a set price (the "strike price") for a certain period of time. If the stock fails to meet the strike price before the expiration date, the option expires worthless. You buy a call option if you think the share price of the underlying security will rise, or sell a call option if you think it will fall. Selling an option is also referred to as "writing" an option. The option seller is called the writer.

Capital

This is a business's cash or property, or an investor's pile of cash. See also: Asset.

Capital appreciation

One of the two components of total return, capital appreciation is how much the underlying value of a security has increased. If you bought a stock at $10 per share and it has risen to $13, you have enjoyed a 30% return or appreciation on the original capital you invested. Dividend yield is the other component of total return.

Capital gain/loss

This is the difference between the price at which an asset is sold and its original purchase price (or "basis").

Capital gains distributions

These are payments, typically made in December, to mutual fund shareholders of gains realized through purchases and sales by the mutual fund during the year. Because these capital gains distributions are sometimes substantial, investors should check with the mutual fund to avoid buying shares of mutual funds just prior to a capital gains distribution.

Capital growth

This is an increase in a stock or bond price. Sometimes called capital appreciation.

Cash account

This is a brokerage account that settles transactions on a cash basis with no opportunity for the account holder to use credit (margin).

Cash and cash equivalents

The first line of a corporate balance sheet is always named this, or some similar phrase. It refers to the amount of money that a company has sitting in the bank. It may also include marketable securities, such as government bonds and banker's acceptances. Cash equivalents on the balance sheet may include securities that mature within 90 days.

Cash flow

This is a measure that tells an investor whether a company is actually bringing cash in to the company's coffers.

Cash flow statement

A financial statement reflecting the monies that go into and out of a business, and the timing of those movements. The cash flow statement reports on cash inflows and outflows in a company's operations, investments, and financing activities.

Cash investments

Short-term debt instruments such as commercial paper and Treasury bills that mature in less than a year. Also known as money market accounts or cash reserves.

Certificate of deposit (CD)

This is an insured, interest-bearing deposit at a bank, requiring the depositor to keep the money invested for a specific length of time.

Certified Financial Planner (CFP)

This is an investment professional who has passed the CFP Board of Standards series of exams on subjects such as taxes, securities, insurance, and estate planning.

Certified Public Accountant (CPA)

This is a professional who is licensed by a state to practice public accounting.

Chairman of the board

This is the head officer of a corporation's board of directors. This person often has executive authority over the company. See also: Board of directors.

Chart

A graph showing how the price of a given stock has changed over time. Other data is often included, such as volume data. Many people claim to be able to divine extraordinary information about the future performance of a stock by consulting charts about the past.

Chartered Financial Analyst (CFA)

This is someone who has passed competency standards -- as determined by the Institute of Chartered Financial Analysts -- in securities, portfolio management, economics, and financial accounting.

Chief Executive Officer (CEO)

The CEO is the highest executive officer in a corporation, sort of like the captain of a ship. He or she is accountable to the company's board of directors and is frequently a member of that board. The CEO participates in setting goals with the board and other officers and is responsible for the strategies and tactics employed to meet the corporation's goals.

Churn

Churning is unconscious or conscious overtrading by a broker in a customer's account. Since the number of transactions made on a customer's behalf most often compensates brokers, there is temptation to trade too frequently, whether in stocks, bonds, or mutual funds with loads.

Closed-end fund

This is a mutual fund that has a fixed number of shares and is typically listed on a major stock exchange. These funds often trade perpetually at a discount to their net asset value (NAV).

Closing price

This is the last trading price of a stock when the market closes for the day.

Commercial paper

This is a promissory note issued by a large company to secure short-term financing.

Commission

A fee charged by a broker for executing a securities transaction. One of the principle things investors should watch for when selecting a brokerage. "Full-service" brokers can have commissions running as high as $150 per trade or more, while discount brokers average less than $20 per trade.

Commodities

Goods such as grains, silver and other precious metals, and minerals traded in large amounts on a commodities exchange.

Common stock

This is a security representing partial ownership in a public or private corporation.

Compounding

When an investment generates earnings on reinvested earnings.

Consumer Price Index (CPI)

This is a method to track inflation that is followed by the mainstream media. It is the measure of the price change in consumer goods and services.

Convertible security

A preferred stock or corporate bond that can be exchanged for shares of the company's common stock at a predetermined price or rate.

Correction

This is a short-term drop in stock market prices. The term "correction" comes from the notion that, when this happens, an overpriced individual stock, market segment, or stocks in general are returning back to their "correct" values.

Cost basis

The original price paid for an investment (including commissions).

Cost/benefit analysis

This is an attempt to determine the feasibility of embarking on a project by quantifying its anticipated costs and benefits.

Coupon/coupon rate

The interest rate that a bond issuer is obligated to pay the bond holder until the bond matures.

Crash

A market crash is a big drop in market value. It is what many shorter-term focused investors always worry about. The stock market never goes up in a straight line, so there will always be crashes. It can take a few days, months, or even years for a market to recover after a crash.

Credit

Money loaned. It also refers to the borrowing capacity of an individual or company.

Credit history

The record of how well an individual or company has, in the past, repaid borrowed money.

Credit limit

This is the maximum amount of money that a bank or other lender will lend to a particular individual or company.

Creditor

This is a person or organization that lends money to others.

Creditworthiness

This is a creditor's measure of a borrower's ability to meet debt obligations.

Cumulative total return

This is the statement of performance of an investment over a stated period of time.

Current assets

These are assets that are easily convertible to cash. Cash, short-term investments, and accounts receivable are asset categories that should result in cash within the next year.

Current liabilities

Debt or other obligations that are payable within a year.

Current ratio

The current ratio provides a quick indication of a company's ability to meet short-term debt obligations. The higher the ratio, the more liquid the company is, and the better able it is to take care of any short-term debt. To determine the ratio, take current assets and divide by current liabilities.

Current yield

As applied to bonds, the annual interest rate divided by the current market price.

Cyclical stock

This is the stock of a company whose performance is generally related (or thought to be related) to the performance of the economy as a whole. Paper, steel, and the automotive stocks are thought to be cyclical because their earnings tend to be hurt when the economy slows and are strong when the economy turns up. Food and drug stocks, on the other hand, are not considered "cyclicals," as consumers pretty much need to eat and care for their health regardless of the performance of the economy.

Daily high

The highest price reached by a stock (or index or commodity) during a given day. See also: Daily low.

Daily low

This is the lowest price to which a stock (or index or commodity) dropped during a given day. See also: Daily high.

Date of record

This is the date on which a company draws up the list of stockholders who will receive a dividend.

Day order

A buy or sell order that, if unfilled, expires automatically at the end of the day on which it was placed. Orders to your broker are day orders unless otherwise specified. See Good-till-canceled order.

Day trader

Day traders are in and out of the market many times during the course of one trading session and often do not hold a position in any stocks overnight. This approach generates a lot of commissions and portfolio turnover, and denies the day trader the ability to participate in the long-term creation of wealth through compounded growth.

Days sales outstanding (DSO)

A measure of how long it takes a company to collect money that it is due. The formula to calculate DSO for one quarter is: accounts receivable / (sales / 90).

Days to cover

A measure of how many shares of a company have been sold short. It is calculated by dividing the number of shares sold short by the average daily trading volume. When you short a stock, you want the days to cover to be low, around seven days or less.

Debenture

This is a debt obligation that is not backed by collateral.

Debt

This is a liability that must be repaid.

Debt-equity swap

A transaction in which a corporation exchanges newly issued stock (equity) for already existing bonds (debt).

Debt-to-equity ratio

Calculated by dividing long-term debt by shareholders' equity. A measure of a company's leverage, this ratio shows the relationship between long-term funds provided by creditors and funds provided by shareholders. A high ratio may indicate high risk, and a low ratio may indicate low risk.

Declaration date

This is the date on which a company's board of directors sets the amount of the next quarterly dividend. Typically it is many weeks in advance of the actual payout date.

Deductible contribution

This is a tax-deductible contribution to a retirement plan.

Default

This is the failure to make a payment, of either principal or interest, when due.

Defined benefit plan

A retirement plan that pays a specified amount to former employees, typically based on the number of years of employment and on the average salary in the years just before retirement. Commonly known as a pension, a defined benefit plan was the predominant way that workers secured their retirement funds prior to the widespread use of defined contribution plans.

Defined contribution plan

This is a retirement plan that is funded by contributions made by the employer and the employee. The ultimate value of the plan will be based on these contributions and on the return of the investments chosen by the plan participant. Profit sharing plans, 401(k)s, 403(b)s, and 457s are defined contribution plans.

Depreciation

This is a decrease in the value of an asset, such as buildings or equipment.

Derivative

This is a financial contract whose value is "derived" from another security, such as stocks, bonds, commodities, or a market index such as the S&P 500 or the Wilshire 5000. The most common types of derivatives are options, futures, and mortgage-backed securities.

Discount broker

A brokerage that executes orders to buy and sell securities at commission rates lower than a full-service brokerage.

Discount rate

The interest rate that is charged by the Federal Reserve Board to member banks for loans.

Distributions

These are withdrawals from a retirement plan or IRA. They are also, payments of dividends and/or capital gains by a mutual fund, which can trigger significant tax consequences for an investor.

Diversification

Investing in separate asset classes (stocks, bonds, cash) and/or stocks of different companies in an attempt to lower overall investment risk.

Dividend

A share of a company's earnings paid to each stockholder. Typically, dividends are paid on a quarterly basis and are determined by the company's board of directors.

Dividend reinvestment plan (Drip)

This is the automatic investment of shareholder dividends into additional shares of the company's stock.

Dividend yield

The annual percentage rate of return paid in dividends on a share of stock. To figure out the dividend yield (or just "yield"), divide the annual dividend by the current share price of the stock.

Dollar cost averaging

Investing equal amounts of money at regular intervals. The money deducted from your paycheck if you participate in your company's 401(k) program is an example of dollar cost averaging. Theoretically, you will buy more shares when the price of your investment has declined, and fewer shares when the price has risen. This may lead to an overall cost basis that is lower than the average price per share.

Dow Jones Industrial Average

The oldest and most widely known index of the U.S. stock market, the Dow represents the price movements of the 30 companies that, in the opinion of the editors of *The Wall Street Journal*, most represent the American economy.

Early withdrawal penalty

A penalty imposed for withdrawing money from a fixed-term investment before the term is complete. For example, cashing in a certificate of deposit (CD) before its maturity triggers an early withdrawal penalty.

Earnings

The money that is left over after a company pays all its bills. Also known as net income or net profit, earnings are reported on a quarterly basis by all publicly traded companies.

Earnings per share (EPS)

This is a company's earnings, also known as net income or net profit, divided by the number of shares outstanding.

Education IRA

A savings account with significant tax advantages designed for use in paying for a child's college education.

Efficient market theory

A theory stating that stock prices perfectly reflect all market information that is known by all investors. The theory also states that no investor can beat the market's returns through skill because it is impossible to determine future stock prices, and that luck explains why some investors beat the market. The theory is much debated.

Emerging markets fund

This is a mutual fund that invests in countries with developing economies such as those in Latin America and Asia (excluding Japan). Emerging markets funds tend to be quite volatile due to political and economic instability.

Employee contribution

This is an employee's deposit to a company retirement plan. Distinguished from the company's contribution, such as a "company match" to a 401(k).

Employee Stock Ownership Plan (ESOP)

This is a retirement plan that invests in the employer's stock for the benefit of employees.

Employer matching contribution

The amount that a company contributes to an employee's retirement account, usually as a "match" of some percentage of the employee's contribution.

Equities

These are shares of stock in a company. Because they represent a proportional share in the business, they are "equitable claims" on the business itself.

Equivalent taxable yield

The yield required from a taxable bond to give the same after-tax yield as a tax-exempt bond.

Estate planning

Estate planning is the preparation of a plan to carry out an individual's wishes as to the disposition of her property before or after her death.

Even lot

This is a grouping of shares of stock divisible by 100 (e.g., 100, 200, 500, 1000).

Ex-dividend date

This is the date during the quarter by which you must own a stock to receive its quarterly dividend payout. The term "ex" means out or without. So, on the ex-date, you buy the stock without the dividend. The company needs some time to get its records straight; it cannot pay the dividend to someone who buys the stock the morning the checks go out.

Expense ratio

The percentage of a mutual fund that is taken out of the pockets of shareholders to pay expenses -- most of which go to the salesmen and managers of the mutual fund.

Federal funds

Federal Reserve deposits that banks and other financial institutions "borrow" from one another to meet short-term cash needs.

Federal funds rate

This is the interest rate that is charged by banks on overnight loans to other banks.

Federal Home Loan Mortgage Corporation ("Freddie Mac")

A publicly traded corporation that provides funds for mortgages, and buys mortgages from banks and re-packages them as mortgage-backed investments.

Federal National Mortgage Association ("Fannie Mae")

A government-sponsored private corporation authorized to purchase and sell mortgages, which increases the affordability and availability of mortgages. Also charged by the federal government with facilitating the orderly operation of a secondary market for home mortgages.

Federal Open Market Committee (FOMC)

This is the 12-member policy-making arm of the Federal Reserve Board. It sets key interest rates, such as the discount rate, and buys and sells government securities, which increases or decreases the nation's money supply.

Federal Reserve

This is the central bank of the United States. The Federal Reserve (or "Fed") oversees money supply, interest rates, and credit. A seven-member board governs the Federal Reserve System. There are 12 regional Federal Reserve Banks and 25 branches in the system.

Fee-only compensation

This is an arrangement in which a financial adviser charges by an hourly rate, or by an agreed upon percentage of assets under management, rather than on a commission basis.

Fiduciary

This is an individual, corporation, or association that is charged with managing or investing another's assets.

FIFO

First in, first out, usually regarding the sale of stock. Unless otherwise specified, the specific shares sold in an account will be the first shares that were bought.

Fiscal year

This is a 12-month accounting period.

Fiscal year-end

This is the end of a 12-month accounting period.

Fixed-income fund

A mutual fund that invests in bonds, CDs, preferred stock, or other fixed-income instruments.

401(k)s, 403(b)s, and 457s

Employer-sponsored retirement plans named after the respective Internal Revenue Code sections in which they appear. Given their tax advantages and the possibility of employer matching (read: FREE MONEY), these plans are well worth considering. For-profit entities offer the 401(k) plan, nonprofits have the almost identical 403(b) plan, and local and state governments offer the 457 plan.

Free cash flow

The cash that's left over after everything -- bills from suppliers, salaries, expenses for the annual holiday bash, new equipment to expand the business -- is said and done.

Theoretically, free cash flow is the amount of cash a business could issue to shareholders in the form of a dividend check.

Front-end load

A sales commission charged by a mutual fund, typically around 5%.

Full-service broker

Full-service brokers earn commissions for each trade made in a customer's account. They make more money by trading in and out of investments. They are sometimes referred to as "full-price brokers." They also typically provide better research than discount brokers.

Fundamental analysis

This is the method of evaluating a company by assessing its financial statements, earnings, sales, and management.

Futures/futures contracts

This is a contract to buy or sell an amount of a commodity for a specific price at a specific point in the future.

Global fund

A mutual fund that invests anywhere in the world, including the U.S.

"Going public"

Performing an initial public offering. That is, offering shares of your company to the public so that they may buy them.

Good-till-canceled (GTC) order

An order to buy or sell a security that remains operative until the order is executed or canceled. This is an order that does not expire if not exercised during the day it is made as with the case of a day order.

Government National Mortgage Association ("Ginnie Mae")

An agency within the U.S. Department of Housing and Urban Development (HUD) that buys mortgages and pools them to form securities that are then sold to investors.

Gross Domestic Product (GDP)

The value of all goods and services provided within the borders of a nation. In the United States, GDP is determined quarterly by the Department of Commerce.

Gross margin

A percentage of how much of each dollar of sales is left over after the costs to make the product are subtracted. It is calculated by dividing gross profits (sales minus cost of goods sold) for a period by the revenues for the same period.

Gross National Product (GNP)

The dollar value of all goods and services produced in a nation's economy. It includes the income from goods and services produced abroad. The GNP adds to the Gross Domestic Product (GDP) of a country the income of domestic residents as a result of investments abroad, and subtracts the income earned in domestic markets that go out to foreigners abroad.

Growth and income fund

This is a mutual fund that pursues long-term growth of capital as well as current dividend income from stocks. This would describe virtually all stock mutual funds to some degree, but the term is used to designate a fund that expressly dedicates a portion of its assets to stocks that pay higher dividends.

Growth stocks

Companies believed to be growing earnings and sales faster than the average company in the market. Growth stocks usually pay little or no dividend, as they are still at a stage in their businesses where they are reinvesting most or all of their earnings into the further development of new areas of the business.

Guaranteed Investment Contract (GIC)

Often a choice for 401(k) plans participants, though not a very good choice for those those who are not close to retirement. A GIC is an agreement between an insurance company and a corporate profit sharing or pension plan that guarantees a specific rate of return over the time span of the agreement.

High-yield bonds

These are bonds that are rated as below investment grade. The issuers of these bonds -- which are judged to be at a higher risk of default -- have to pay an attractive dividend to compensate investors for the additional risk.

High-yield fund

This is a mutual fund that invests in bonds with low credit ratings. Because of the risky nature of high-yield bonds, high-yield funds have greater volatility than the average bond fund.

Income fund

This is a mutual fund that invests in bonds and stocks with higher-than-average dividends.

Index

This is an unmanaged selection of securities whose collective performance is used as a standard to measure investment results. Examples include the Dow Jones Industrial Average, the Standard & Poor's 500, and the Wilshire 5000.

Index fund

This is a passively managed mutual fund that seeks to match the performance of a particular market index. Partially due to lower expenses, index funds outperform the majority of actively managed mutual funds.

Individual Retirement Account (IRA)

A tax-deferred retirement account set up with a financial institution such as a bank, broker, or mutual fund in which contributions may be invested in many types of securities such as stocks, bonds, money market funds, CDs, etc.

Inflation

This is a rise in the prices of goods and services.

Initial public offering (IPO)

A company's first offering of common stock to the public.

Insider trading

Trading done by a person with access to key non-public information.

Institution investors

Institutions investors include pension funds, insurance funds, mutual funds, and hedge funds. Although institutions hold about 40% to 50% of all stock owned, they account for as much as 90% of daily trading volume.

International fund

A mutual fund that invests in securities traded in foreign markets.

Inventory

This is finished or near-finished products that a company has not yet sold. It's considered an asset because it can be sold or liquidated for money.

Investment adviser

This is an entity that makes the recommendations and/or decisions regarding a portfolio's investments. Alternatively called a portfolio manager.

Investment grade

This is a bond whose credit quality is considered to be among the most secure by any independent bond-rating agency. A rating of Baa or higher by Moody's Investors Service or a rating of BBB or higher by Standard & Poor's is considered investment grade.

Keogh plan

A qualified retirement plan that may be set up by self-employed persons, partnerships, and owners of unincorporated businesses as either a defined benefit or defined contribution plan. As defined contribution plans, they may be structured as a profit sharing, a money purchase, or a combined profit sharing/money purchase plan.

Large-capitalization ("large-cap") stocks

Large caps are stocks of companies whose market value is above a designated minimum, usually in the neighborhood of $10 billion.

Liabilities

Outstanding debts.

Limit order

This is an order to buy or to sell a security at a specific price or better.

Liquidity

This is a measure of how quickly a stock can be sold at a fair price and converted to cash. Illiquid stocks are stocks that don't trade in high volume. Thus, having too many shares of a stock that doesn't trade frequently would make for a position that cannot necessarily be sold.

Load

A sales commission paid when purchasing shares of a mutual fund (called a front-end load) or when redeeming shares of a mutual fund (called a back-end load). For example, if the fund has a front-end load of 5%, for every $100 you place into the fund, only $95 is invested, with $5 going to the salesperson and/or mutual fund company. Avoid mutual funds with loads.

Long-term capital gain

A profit on the sale of stock, mutual fund shares, or other securities that have been held for more than one year. Taxes owed on long-term capital gains are lower than those on short-term capital gains.

Long-term assets

A long-term asset is one that is consumed or used over a number of accounting cycles, from more than one year to 40 years. The long-term asset accounts include assets such as land, buildings, equipment, and intangibles such as goodwill and accrued organizational expenses. It appears on the balance sheet.

Lump-sum distribution

This is a single payment that amounts to the entirety of a retiree's interest in a qualified retirement plan. Severe tax consequences apply to receiving a lump-sum distribution without retiring (or otherwise being separated from employment).

Management fee

The money paid to the manager(s) of a mutual fund, annuity subaccount, or other type of professionally managed investment. Also called an advisory fee.

Margin account

This is a brokerage account that permits the owner to borrow money to buy securities.

Margin call

This is a brokerage firm's demand that a customer deposit enough money or securities to bring a margin account back up to the minimum maintenance amount. This is typically made after the value of the margined securities has plummeted.

Market capitalization (market cap)

A company's total stock market value, calculated by multiplying the price of a single share by the total number of shares outstanding. You can find information about shares outstanding from the company's last quarterly report or any online quote service.

Market order

This is an order to buy or sell immediately at the best price available.

Market timing

An investment strategy based on predicting short-term price changes in securities, which is virtually impossible to do.

Maturity/maturity date

This is the date on which the issuer of a certificate of deposit or a bond agrees to repay the principal to the buyer.

Merger

This is the unification of two or more companies.

Micro-cap stock

Stocks with market capitalization of less than $150 million.

Mid-capitalization (mid-cap) stocks

These are companies whose market value is between $1 billion and about $10 billion.

Money market fund

This is a mutual fund that invests in very short-term, high-liquidity investments. Similar to a savings account, though usually offering better interest rates.

Municipal bond

This is a debt instrument issued by a state or local government. The advantage of investing in municipal bonds (or "munis") is their exemption from federal, and sometimes state and local, taxes.

Municipal bond fund

This is a mutual fund that invests primarily in municipal bonds.

Mutual fund

The pooled cash of many shareholders that is invested according to a stated objective, as defined by the fund's prospectus.

Mutual savings bank

This is a savings bank that is owned by, and operated for the benefit of, its depositors.

Naked options

These are options that are sold on securities when the seller does not actually own shares of the underlying securities -- a highly risky endeavor. Naked options are also referred to as "uncovered options."

NASD Regulation (NASDR)

This is an independent subsidiary of the NASD that regulates the activities of broker/dealers in the over-the-counter markets and the Nasdaq Stock Market.

Nasdaq (National Association of Securities Dealers Automated Quotations)

A computerized system that stores and displays up-to-the-second price quotations for securities traded over the counter.

Nasdaq 100 Index

This is an index that includes the Nasdaq's 100 largest companies (Microsoft, Intel, WorldCom, Dell, etc.) and is heavily focused on technology companies. You can buy it as a single stock.

National Association of Investors Corporation (NAIC)

The NAIC is a nonprofit association dedicated to the education of investment clubs and individuals.

National Association of Securities Dealers (NASD)

This is the largest securities-industry self-regulatory organization in the United States. Through its subsidiaries -- the NASD Regulation, Inc. and The Nasdaq Stock Market, Inc. -- the National Association of Securities Dealers develops rules and regulations and conducts regulatory reviews of members' business activities.

<u>Net asset value (NAV)</u>

This is the price of each share of a mutual fund. Subtracting the fund's liabilities from its total assets, and dividing that figure by the number of shares outstanding calculate it. The NAV is the amount of money that an investor would receive for each share if the mutual fund sold all of its assets, paid off all of its outstanding debts, and distributed the proceeds to shareholders.

Net income

Gross income minus total expenses gives you net income. You'll find this information on the income statement.

Net investment

Gross, or total, investment minus depreciation.

Net profit

This is how much money the company made in profits. It can also refer to net profit margin, which is a percentage telling you how many cents on each dollar is pure profit.

<u>Net profit margin</u>

This is net income as a percentage of sales. You get this by dividing net income by sales. Since it's a percentage, it tells you how many cents on each dollar of sales is pure profit.

Net quick assets

Cash, accounts receivable (which is money owed to the company from its customers), and marketable securities, minus current liabilities.

Net revenue

Net revenue is sales less returns, discounts, and allowances.

New York Stock Exchange (NYSE)

The oldest and largest stock exchange in the United States, this Wall Street haunt is frequently featured on television, with hundreds of traders on the floor staring up at screens and answering phones, ready to trade stocks on command from their firms.

Nikkei Index

An index of more than 200 blue-chip stocks traded on the Tokyo Stock Exchange.

No-load fund

This is a mutual fund that does not charge a sales commission.

Nominal returns

Investment returns before adjusting for inflation.

Odd lot

Trading securities in share amounts of either less than 100 or an amount that is not a multiple of 100. Trading in odd lots used to incur higher transaction fees from full-service brokerages. Today, with online, computerized discount trading, buying and selling stock in odd lots no longer involves higher transaction costs.

One-time charge

A cost that a company must pay once, as compared with costs it must pay regularly. If, for instance, the company spends money to acquire another company, that may be considered a "one-time charge." One-time charges are generally backed out of earnings for comparisons to prior time periods so that they don't artificially inflate or deflate the company's performance.

Open order

A buy or sell order that has not yet been canceled or executed.

Open-end fund

This is a mutual fund that has an unlimited number of shares available for purchase. Most mutual funds are open-ended. See Closed-end fund.

Operating cash flow

Cash accumulates in the course of a company running its business.

Operating cycle

The time it takes to sell a product and collect cash from the sale. An operating cycle can last from several weeks to a number of years.

Operating expenses

This is the cost of doing business. Operating expenses are deducted from revenues, and the result is, hopefully, profits.

Option

A call option is a contract in which a seller gives a buyer the right, but not the obligation, to buy the optioned shares of a company at a set price (the strike price) for a certain period of time. If the stock fails to exceed the strike price before the expiration date, the option expires worthless. A put option is a contract that gives the buyer the right, but not the obligation, to sell the stock underlying the contract at a predetermined price (the strike price). The seller (or writer) of the put option is obligated to buy the stock at the strike price.

Order

This is a request from a client to a broker to buy or sell stock, either at the market price or at a specific price.

Over the counter (OTC)

This is a geographically decentralized market in which stock and other securities transactions are not conducted in person -- as on the much-televised floor of the New York Stock Exchange -- but through a telephone and computer network. The National Association of Securities Dealers (NASD) regulates the over-the-counter market.

Owner Earnings Run Rate

Net income + Depreciation +/- One Time Events - Capital Expenditures

Par value (bond)

The stated value of a bond as printed on its certificate or the amount the issuer must repay when the bond reaches maturity. A par bond is one selling at its face value.

Par value (stock)

This is an arbitrary dollar value that a company assigns to its shares. Par value has no economic significance. The legal significance of par value is, roughly, that if shares are issued below par value, the holders of those shares might be assessed the difference between par value and the issue price. Most stock certificates state that the shares are fully paid and nonassessable to indicate that holders are not on the hook for additional contributions because the shares were issued at a price greater than par value. Companies usually assign a very low par value to common stock.

Payment date

This is the date that dividend checks go out.

Penny stock

A very cheap, speculative stock, selling for less than $1 a share, though the term is sometimes applied to stocks selling for up to $5 a share.

Portfolio

All the securities held by an individual, institution, or mutual fund.

Portfolio manager

This is any individual(s) in charge of the investment decisions for a portfolio.

Power of attorney

This is a legal agreement that authorizes a specific individual to handle certain decisions for another. There are two types of power of attorney: limited and full. A limited power of attorney might permit one to engage in transactions in a specific investment account. A full power of attorney could allow more enhanced authority, including transferring funds between accounts.

Preferred stock

Preferred stock pays a dividend on a regular schedule and is given preference over common stock in regard to the payment of dividends or any liquidation of the company. Their share prices tend to remain stable, and will generally not carry the voting right that common stock does.

Pretax contribution

A contribution to a retirement account (such as a 401(k)) with money from your paycheck before the federal government takes its cut. Pretax contributions reduce your taxable pay and, therefore, reduce the taxes withheld from your paycheck.

Price-to-book ratio

Shareholders' equity divided by the number of shares of stock outstanding.
Price-to-earnings ratio (P/E)

The share price of a stock, divided by its per-share earnings over the past year.

Prime rate

The interest rate that lenders charge their very best, most-reliable customers.

Principal

The original cash put into an investment.

Proceeds

The cash received from selling an investment. Net proceeds are the cash pocketed after subtracting the purchase price, including all fees and commissions.

Pro forma

The financial statements of a company that are adjusted to reflect a projected or recently completed transaction. For example, pro forma results are used to show the earnings that newly merged companies might have achieved had the merger occurred at the beginning of the reporting period. The term may be applied to income statements, balance sheets, and statements of cash flow. Pro forma quarterly results can sometimes be confusing, as they may exclude information such as certain stock-based employee compensation costs.

Property, plant, and equipment (PP&E)

This is the original cost of assets, less their accumulated depreciation. Often called fixed assets. Accounting does not normally use market prices, either selling prices or replacement costs, for fixed assets. Reasons may be that the company usually does not intend to sell these assets, so their market resale prices are not relevant; original cost is a verifiable, objective number, while market prices (selling or buying) fluctuate; and financial statements portray the stewardship of the managers, so it is natural to show how they spent the money entrusted to them by shareholders.

Prospectus

A legal document usually written in extraordinarily tedious language that provides information about a potential investment, including discussions of its investment objectives, policies, past performance, risks, and cost.

Put

A put option is a contract that gives the buyer the right, but not the obligation, to sell the stock underlying the contract at a predetermined price (the strike price). The seller (or writer) of the put option is obligated to buy the stock at the strike price. Put options can be exercised at any time before the option expires.

Qualified retirement plan

A retirement plan sponsored by a business for its employees, such as a 401(k) or a 403(b). Contributions are pre-tax, and the earnings grow tax-deferred. Any withdrawals made before age 59 1/2 will usually be penalized. To be qualified, the plan must be open to all employees.

Quarter

Businesses have four quarters equal to three months, in every fiscal year. After each quarter, a company is required to file a report with the SEC providing investors with juicy details about the company's performance.

Quick ratio

Current assets minus inventories divided by current liabilities. By taking inventories out of the equation, you can check and see if a company has sufficient liquid assets to meet short-term operating needs.

Quotation

This is the price being bid (by a prospective buyer) or offered (by a potential seller) for a stock.

Real estate investment trust (REIT)

REITs are a specialized form of equity that allows investors to own a portion of a group of real estate properties, although many investors think of them as an alternative to bonds. Granted special tax status by the Internal Revenue Service, REITs pay out at least 95% of their earnings in the form of dividends to shareholders, often offering healthy dividend yields of the same magnitude as bonds. As REITs acquire more property and increase the value of the properties they own, the value of the equity may increase as well.

Real return

This is the inflation-adjusted return of an investment. For example, the returns for stocks during the 20th century were approximately 11% annually. However, that does not factor in the roughly 3% annual inflation rate over the same time period. Therefore, the real return of stocks was approximately 8% annually.

Real yield

Since the interest payment on an individual bond is the same every year, the bond's future payments are worth less and less as inflation erodes the value of the dollar.

Record date

The date on which a company's books are closed in order to identify share owners and distribute quarterly dividends, proxies, or other financial documentation.

Reinvestment

This is the use of investment income or dividends to buy additional shares.

Relative strength

Relative strength rates the performance of every stock listed on the three major U.S. exchanges (the New York Stock Exchange, the American Stock Exchange, and the Nasdaq). The rating system gives a numerical grade to the performance of a stock over the past 12 months, assigning a grade of 1 to 99. Thus, relative strength is a momentum indicator. A relative strength of 95, for example, indicates a wonderful stock that has outperformed 95% of all other stocks over the past year.

Research and development (R&D)

An expense reported on the income statement, reflecting the company's effort to discover and invest in new technologies.

Retained earnings

Income a company has earned, less the dividends it has paid. The key is the word "retained," which implies that income remains in the business, rather than being distributed to stockholders as dividends.

Return on equity (ROE)

Return on equity is a measure of how much in earnings a company generates in four quarters compared to its shareholders' equity. It is measured as a percentage. For instance, if XYZ Corp. made $1 million in the past year and has shareholders' equity of $10 million, then the ROE is 10%. Some use ROE as a screen to find companies that can generate large profits with little in the way of capital investment.

Return on invested capital

Return on invested capital (ROIC) is a measure of financial performance and a financial performance-forecasting tool.

Revenue

This is money that a company collects from customers for the sale of a product or service. When you subtract out all costs from revenues, you get profits or earnings.

Reverse split

This is a stock split that reduces the number of outstanding shares and proportionately increases the price per share. If there was a "one-for-ten" reverse split. For every ten shares you owned, you would now be left with one. Meanwhile, the share price is increased tenfold. If yesterday you owned 100 shares at $5 each, today you own 10 shares at $50 each. The value is still $500.

Risk tolerance

This is the measurement of an investor's willingness to suffer a decline (or repeated declines) in the value of investments while waiting and hoping for them to increase in value.

Risk-adjusted return

A measure of how much risk a portfolio has employed to earn its returns.

Rollover

Moving all or a portion of tax-deferred retirement plans savings into another plan (e.g., moving 401(k) assets into an IRA).

Rollover IRA

This is a traditional individual retirement account holding money from a qualified plan, such as a 401(k).

Roth IRA

An individual retirement account to which contributions are not tax-deductible. Withdrawals from the account are tax-free.

Round lot

A group of shares traded in multiples of 100.

Russell 2000

A market-cap weighted index that serves as the benchmark for U.S. small-cap stocks.

Salary Reduction Simplified Employee Pension Plan (SARSEP)

Prior to January 1, 1997, a SEP-IRA could have included a salary reduction arrangement in which an employee may elect to defer taxation on part of his or her compensation by contributing that amount to the SEP. This type of salary reduction plan is known as a SARSEP, and could have been established by an employer who had fewer than 25 employees provided at least 50% of all employees agreed to participate in the arrangement. Like a 401(k) plan, the employee's contribution to the SARSEP is limited to $10,500 per year. Effective January 1, 1997, no new SARSEP may be established; however, those in existence as of December 31, 1996, may continue to operate.

Same-store sales

Also called comparable-store sales (or simply "comps", same-store sales measure the percentage change in revenues for all stores in the chain that have been open more than one year.

Savings Incentive Match Plan for Employees (SIMPLE)

Established by the Small Business Protection Act of 1996, a SIMPLE may be set up by employers who have no other retirement plan and who have 100 or fewer employees with at least $5,000 in compensation for the previous year. SIMPLE plans are the replacement for the SARSEP plans discussed above. They may be structured as an IRA or as a 401(k) plan. Employees may defer any percentage of compensation up to $6,000 per year to the SIMPLE, and the employer is required to make a matching contribution of up to 3% of the employee's pay based on that election. The employer may reduce the maximum matching percentage in any two years out of five. Alternatively, the employer may establish a uniform 2% of salary contribution per year for all eligible employees regardless of whether they contribute to the SIMPLE or not. Together, the employee and the employer may contribute a maximum of $12,000 annually to the SIMPLE. \

Secondary offering

This is the sale of a large block of company stock anytime after the initial public offering. The stock can come from company officials, institutions with a lot of shares, or the offering company itself in the form of brand-new shares.

Sector

This is a group of companies that have shared characteristics, usually operating in a common industry.

Sector fund

This is a mutual fund that invests its shareholders' money in a relatively narrow market sector, e.g., technology, energy, the Internet, or banking.

Securities

A term used for shares of stock, bonds, or any kind of financial asset that can be traded.

Securities and Exchange Commission (SEC)

The federal agency charged with ensuring that the U.S. stock market is a free and open market. All companies with stock registered in the United States must comply with SEC rules and regulations, which include filing quarterly reports on how the company is doing.

Settlement date

This is the date by which a broker must receive payment to satisfy the terms of a security transaction. The settlement date for stocks is three business days from the execution of the trade.

Shareholder

If you buy even one share of stock in a company, you can proudly call yourself a shareholder. As a shareholder you get an invitation to the company's annual meeting, and you have the right to vote on the members of the board of directors and other company matters.

Short sale

An investor who sells stock short borrows shares from a brokerage house and sells them to another buyer. Proceeds from the sale go into the shorter sellers account. He must buy those shares back (cover) at some point in time and return them to the lender.

Short squeeze

When many investors have sold short a stock on the hope that its price will plunge, price may begin to rise. As it does so, more and more of these people will "cover" their investments. That is, they'll buy back the shares that they had shorted, and take a loss, since they're buying the shares at a higher price. As more and more people do this, the price rises (since more people are buying than selling).

Short-term capital gain

This is the profit on the sale of a security that has been held for one year or less. Short-term capital gains are taxed as ordinary income.

Short-term reserves

These are investments in U.S. Treasury bills, money market instruments, interest-bearing bank deposits, or short-term bonds.

Simplified Employee Pension (SEP) plan

A SEP is an easy method for a small employer to establish a retirement plan for employees without the complex administration and expense found in qualified retirement plans. In fact, an employer may establish a SEP only if that employer has no qualified retirement plan in effect. Under a SEP, the employer may make a contribution of up to the lesser of 15% or $30,000 of compensation to IRAs established in each employee's name.

Small-capitalization ("small-cap") fund

A mutual fund that invests in companies whose market value is less than about $1 billion.

Small-capitalization ("small-cap") stocks

These are companies with a market capitalization of $1 billion or less.

Spiders

This is the nickname for S&P 500 Depositary Receipts, which trade on the American Stock Exchange under the ticker symbol SPY. Spiders are a convenient way for investors to buy and sell the aggregate stock of the companies represented in the S&P 500 Index.

Spousal IRA

An IRA funded by a married taxpayer in the name of his or her spouse who has less than $250 in annual compensation. The couple must file a joint tax return for the year of contribution. The working spouse may contribute up to $2,000 per year to the Spousal IRA and up to $2,000 per year to his or her own IRA. A couple, then, may contribute up to $4,000 per year provided neither IRA receives more than $2,000.

Spread

The difference between the bid and ask price, i.e., the highest price offered and the lowest priced asked for a security.

Standard & Poor's 500 Index

An index of 500 of the biggest publicly traded companies in the United States. The S&P 500 is generally thought of as the best measurement of the overall U.S. stock market.

Standard & Poor's MidCap 400 Index

A market-capitalization-weighted index composed of exactly 400 companies (thus the name) with market values between roughly $200 million and $5 billion.

Stock

An ownership share in a corporation. Each share of stock is a proportional stake in the corporation's assets and profits, and purchasing a stock should be thought of as owning a proportional share of the successes and failures of that business.

Stock certificate

This is a document designating and verifying shareholder ownership in a corporation.

Stock fund

This is a mutual fund investing primarily in stocks.

Stock split

A stock split simply involves a company altering the number of its shares outstanding and proportionally adjusting the share price to compensate.

Stock broker

An individual who has been licensed by the National Association of Securities Dealers to trade stocks and advise clients on various personal finance issues.

Street name

Registration of securities held in the name of the owner's broker to facilitate share transfers at the time of sale.

Taxable equivalent yield

This is the return from a higher-paying but taxable investment that would be equivalent to the return from a tax-free investment. To determine this, you need to know the tax bracket of the individual paying the taxes on the income.

Taxable year

The 12 months used by an individual to report income for income tax purposes. For most, but not all, this will simply be the calendar year.

Tax-deferred

These are accounts in which taxes are not paid on investment growth or earnings until funds are withdrawn from the account, such as an Individual Retirement Account or a 401(k) plan.

Tax-deferred retirement plan

Any retirement plan such as a 401(k) in which earnings are not currently taxable.

Tax-exempt bond

This is a bond -- typically issued by state, county, or municipal governments -- whose interest payments are not taxed by the federal government. These bonds may or may not be subject to state and local income taxes.

Tax-sheltered

This is an investment exempt from federal and, in some cases, state or local income taxes.

Technical analysis

Technical analysis studies charts of stock price movements and trading volume, as opposed to a company's business, earnings, and competition.

Term insurance

This is a no-nonsense life insurance plan that calls for low annual payments ("premiums") that will increase, as you get older. See also Whole life insurance.

Ticker symbol

An abbreviation for a company's name that is used as shorthand by stock-quote reporting services and brokerages.

Top line

The top line on a business' income statement shows its sales, otherwise known as revenues.

Trade

This is the purchase or sale of a stock, bond, or other security.

Trading range

This is the upper and lower selling price of a security over a given time period, such as the last 52 weeks.

Traditional IRA

An Individual Retirement Account in which contributions may be deductible, non-deductible, or both.

Transaction fee

A charge assessed by a broker for assisting in the trade of a stock or other security.

Treasury bill (T-bill)

A short-term discounted security issued by the U.S. government, with maturity of one year or less.

Treasury bond (T-bond)

A long-term security issued by the U.S. government, with a maturity of 10 years or more.

Treasury note (T-note)

This is an intermediate-term security issued by the U.S. government, having a maturity of 1 to 10 years.

Turnover rate

This is a measurement of trading activity during the past year. Mutual funds with lower turnover rates will leave their shareholders with lower tax bills at the end of the year.

12b-1 fee

This is the cost of mutual fund promotional expenses such as advertising and public relations that are paid by shareholders.

Underwriter

A brokerage firm that helps a company go public in an initial public offering. The firm underwrites (vouches for) the stock. When a company has been brought public, the shares have been underwritten. See Initial public offering.

Uniform Gifts to Minors Act (UGMA)

A law adopted by many states that provides a method for giving irrevocable gifts to children while maintaining custodial control over the account. You or some other custodian who acts on behalf of a minor manage UGMA accounts. Eventually (at an age of 18 to 25, depending on the state) the assets have to be turned over to the child.

Uniform Transfers to Minors Act (UTMA)

Similar to the Uniform Gifts to Minors Act, this law permits the transfer of gifts in addition to cash and securities (such as real estate or art) to children, while maintaining custodial control over the account.

Unit investment trust (UIT)

An investment usually sold by brokers that purchases a fixed, unmanaged portfolio of stocks or other securities, and then sells shares in the trust to investors, usually in units of at least $1,000.

Unrealized capital gain/loss

This is an increase (or decrease) in the value of a stock or other security that is not "realized" because the security has not yet been sold for a gain or loss.

Utility

This is a business that provides a service essential to almost everyone. Electric companies, natural gas providers, and local phone companies are often referred to as utilities.

Value stocks

Stocks that have a lower-than-average price as measured by such metrics as price-to-earnings or price-to-book ratios. Value investing is often considered the opposite of growth investing, which concentrates on finding companies with above-average sales and earnings growth prospects.

Variable annuity

A variable annuity allows an investor to choose from a range of mutual fund look-alikes, called "sub-accounts." they often carry the same name and are operated by the same investment managers as publicly offered mutual funds, and they will typically offer a selection of stock, bond, and money market sub-account investments.

Volatility

This is the degree of movement in the price of a stock or other security.

Volume

This is the amount (expressed in shares or dollars) of a stock that is traded during a specified period.

Wall Street

The main street in New York City's financial district, although the term is used mostly to refer to the establishment of investing professionals, frequently referred to as "The

Wise." The street is so named because it was once the site of a wall built in the 1600s by the Dutch to protect what was then New Amsterdam.

Warrant

This is an entitlement to purchase a certain number of shares of stock at a predetermined price (usually higher than the current price) for an extended period of time. Typically, warrants are offered with a bond issue or an IPO.

Wash sale rule

Under the wash sale rules, if you sell stock for a loss and buy it back within the 30 days, the loss cannot be claimed for tax purposes. This rule is designed to prevent taxpayers from selling stock to claim the loss while buying it back within a short period to retain ownership. Note that the rule applies to a 30-day period before or after the sale date to prevent "buying the stock back" before it's even sold.

Whole life insurance

This is a life insurance product with an investment component.

Wilshire 4500 Equity Index

A benchmark index made up of the Wilshire 5000 Equity Index, excluding the Standard & Poor's 500 Index. For those who own only or primarily S&P index funds, purchasing shares of the Wilshire 4500 would provide exposure to the rest of the market.

Wilshire 5000 Equity Index

A benchmark index made up of all U.S. stocks regularly traded on the three major U.S. exchanges (the New York Stock Exchange, the American Stock Exchange, and the Nasdaq).

Withdrawal

This is money taken out of an account.

Working capital

This is money a company has readily available for use. Take the total current assets and subtract the total current liabilities. In calculating a company's working capital, you compare money the company has at its disposal to money it needs to pay out in the near future.

Yield (or dividend yield)

This is the income relative to the current share price that a company will pay out to the shareholders on a regular basis, usually expressed in percentage terms.

Yield curve

A line plotted on a graph that depicts the yields of bonds of varying maturities, from short-term to long-term. The line, or "curve," shows the relationship between short- and long-term interest rates.

Zero-coupon bond

These bonds are so named because the coupon rate (the amount of interest paid) is zero. Rather than paying interest on a periodic basis, these bonds are issued at a fraction of their par value and increase in value as they approach maturity (e.g., U.S. savings bonds).